THE COMMON SENSE

NO-FRILLS, PLAIN-ENGLISH GUIDE

TO BEING A SUCCESSFUL DAD

To Carolyn

Best regards,

Ron Klinger

THE COMMON SENSE
NO-FRILLS, PLAIN-ENGLISH GUIDE
TO BEING A SUCCESSFUL

{that every mother should read too}

by Ronald L. Klinger, Ph.D.
with Gay Klinger, M.S.

CSF PUBLISHING

Printed in the United States of America

CSF PUBLISHING
13740 Research Boulevard, Suite G4
Austin, Texas, 78750

Cover and book design by Buds Design Kitchen, Austin, Texas
The typeface used for the book is Minion, created by Robert Slimbach
Text paper is Champion Carnival Vellum

Library of Congress Cataloging in Publication Data:

Klinger, Ronald L.
The Common Sense No-Frills, Plain-English Guide to Being a
Successful Dad / Ronald L. Klinger, Ph.D.–1st ed.
140 pp.   cm
                    306.8742KL   96-94881
                                            CIP
ISBN: 0-9654886-0-8

Acknowledgments

This book reflects beliefs and values that are anchored firmly within my experience. The process that I undertook to interview active fathers verified and strengthened those beliefs and encouraged me to share with other less confident men the time tested contributions of fathers.

It was not until I began to actually teach young fathers about being fathers that I realized the depths at which these lessons touched. Over and again at workshops fathers told me stories of their own fathers and grandfathers, important men stored within their memories. My talks triggered their recollections about fathering. By attaching my words to their experiences, familiar common sense patterns reemerged like forgotten treasures, which once recovered are viewed with renewed value and honor.

To my father Marvin, my grandfathers Walter and Albert and my Uncle Reagan I acknowledge your contributions and thank you. All were true men, world-hardened and caring. These men set the template for masculine parenting within my memory.

Within more recent times others have offered support and opened doorways. Carol Pearson's books and our personal conversations greatly influenced and motivated me to step forward and say aloud what I believed. Thanks also to Marvin Allen for allowing me to "test" my notions about fathering at the International Men's Conferences.

Kathy Armenta stands out as a major source of support. Kathy, a school social worker, was the first to recognize the importance fathers could make within her school. For long years, Kathy and I experimented with ways to capture and hold the interest of young fathers. Kathy made it happen.

Thanks to Terry Bell, Don Horton, Eric Whitfield and Thad Gillespie, all friends of the Center for Successful Fathering, who said, "Write the book!" To Bill Hallett for hours, days, months of working and reworking this material. My sincere and grateful thanks.

Emilie Bell offered her editorial assistance and insights. Susan Reed's support throughout the process added immeasurably to my efforts to bring the book to life. I am indebted to each of you.

My wife and life companion Gay not only contributed to the book, but withstood my grumpy attitudes over the past year. Finally to Christopher, my son, whose insistence on being himself kindled the awaking of my awareness as his father. My thanks, admiration and love to both of you.

Contents

Introduction

Who is this book written for, really? Actually, I did not set out to write a book at all. My intent was to design a training program for fathers of young children. By young children, I mean elementary school aged and younger. As it turns out, not all fathers of young children are young fathers themselves. Of course, many new dads are relatively young, but I was forty years old when my son was born in 1983.

Many of the older fathers were starting their second families and really wanted to make up for past mistakes the second time around. At the same time, there were many younger dads who seemed to be very career oriented and prone to spending a lot of time at work or on the road.

In many, many instances, fathers would ask me if I had gotten "the stuff" I had been talking about in the workshops from a currently available book. When I told them the "stuff" was "my stuff" and asked why they needed such a book, their answers surprised me.

I discovered, happily, that many of the fathers were sharing the fathering issues we had discussed with their wives. "This is a good thing," I told myself. Their wives, I learned however, often did not believe the things I was saying. Arguments had occurred. The men wanted a book, authored by a person of high esteem, to fortify their assertions that fathers can indeed play unique roles in the lives of their children. "This is not so good," I told myself, worriedly.

Still, I did not choose to write a book. I instead invited mothers to attend the fathering sessions. Many accepted the invitation. Some, I believe, may have come prepared to quarrel with me, although none did. "How about this?" I thought. Other mothers came with their husbands and talked (often more than the dads wanted them to, I fear), but their posture was curiously supportive, although at times challenging.

I have come to believe from these experiences that many of today's mothers have not had active fathers in their lives. Others had fathers who abandoned their families or allowed themselves to be driven off as a consequence of divorce. Though some mothers are initially defensive about the prospect of fathers invading their territory, I have found that a majority of mothers want what is best for their kids, and if that includes pulling dad in on the parenting act, they are willing to consider the proposition. Many of these women have also suggested that I produce reading materials to accompany the workshops and to frame my thoughts in such a way to make them accessible to both moms and dads.

Mothers want what is best for their kids, and if that includes pulling dad in on the parenting act, they are willing to consider the proposition.

So I have written this book. I have brought it directly from my instructional sessions. I am aiming at fathers of young children, though, importantly, it is not for men only! In fact, I have included spaces throughout the text for mothers to make their notes, jot down points on which they disagree, personal anecdotes and questions to explore with their husbands.

HOW CAN YOU DECIDE IF THE BOOK IS WORTH READING?

To help answer this question, consider how I decided to create the fathering training program in the first place. I have already mentioned that I am a father. I am a family psychologist as well, so I have a dual interest in both fathering issues and family relationships.

While I began in earnest to collect my thoughts about fathering and sequence them as a fathering curriculum in the Spring of 1994, my work with fathers started much earlier, in the late 1980's. At the urging of my friend, Kathy Armenta, who is a social worker at an elementary school, I agreed to lead a "support group" for fathers in the Fall of 1991.

I discovered at the first session that the dads were going to have considerable difficulty connecting with the typical support group format. To say that they were not exactly comfortable with the notion of sharing their inadequacies as fathers with each other would be a gross understatement. Although the support group was a dud, I became determined to find out what it was these dads needed to learn but for which they could not ask for.

On the assumption that people enjoy being asked their opinions, I called a moratorium on the support group idea. Instead, I began asking fathers all the questions I could think of about fathering. Before long, I had collected tons of responses; but, to be honest, I wondered if I was really learning anything I could use.

One night, as I talked with a small group of fathers in an otherwise empty school, I came up with the question that was to dramatically change the direction of my work. Perhaps it was the way I framed the question, but it totally paralyzed the fathers. Previously animated and talkative, they acted as if I had splashed them with liquid nitrogen. They sat frozen and mute. It was amazing. As I stood looking on, it dawned on me that their silence was telling me where my work should lead!

I am certain that the same question can help you decide if this book is personally worth reading. If you answer the question thoroughly and well, then the contents of the book may be a verification of what you have already come to understand. My insights will probably seem like common sense observations, which fundamentally they are. If my question causes you to stumble or go blank, then probably you have come to the right place. So, here is the question:

Beyond wage earning, what are the unique contributions that fathers give their children?

This is not a trick question, nor is it rhetorical. I have found that active fathers offer their children irreplaceable contributions, and if you are a father, it will make your job a lot easier if you are familiar with the obligations that come with the territory. List the ones you can think of below:

Beyond wage earning, what are the unique contributions that fathers give their children?

_____

_____

_____

_____

_____

_____

_____

I have collected 13 of these contributions through my interviews with successful fathers. While there is nothing magical about the exact number of contributions fathers make, if you think of only a handful, then I suggest you do not put the book down just yet.

WHAT EXACTLY DOES THIS BOOK COVER?

In the strictest sense, this is not a "How To" book. Do not expect to find 101 tips on things dads can do with their little girls. It has been my experience that men in general and fathers in particular typically resent having someone attempt to micro-manage how they do their job or run their lives.

The aim of this book is to point dads in the right direction, with a conceptual road map to guide the way. I have organized the issues I want to talk about into relatively brief "chunks" that are more or less free standing. If you are like me, you wedge your reading time in between many other activities that compete for your attention. It is my intent that the reader can pick up this book, read enough to capture an idea, then move on. Later, at another reading opportunity, the reader may quickly digest the next chunk. After the upcoming chapter, "Who Needs a Dad Anyway?", the book can be read in any order the reader chooses. Here is an overview of the "chunks."

WHO NEEDS A DAD ANYWAY?

Americans no longer believe that fathers are essential... beyond paying the bills!

Over the past 30 plus years, fathers have played an increasingly diminishing parenting role in their children's upbringing. Divorce, alcoholism, career and economic demands and a host of other factors have dramatically cut away at the influence fathers have on their offspring. Thirty-five years without fathers has resulted in a restructuring of our national belief system at both personal and cultural levels. Many Americans no longer believe that fathers are essential...beyond paying the bills! The belief that fathers are expendable is extremely powerful in directing decisions that affect our children's lives and the future of our country. This belief is wrong and I will tell you why fathers are irreplaceable.

ABSENT DADS, LOST KIDS

This is the bad news. If you like horror movies, you will love this stuff. Based largely on data compiled by the National Fatherhood Initiative, I have compressed the information into a brief but frightening package. You will find this information in the second section of the book.

WHAT'S A FATHER TO DO?

This is the good news and the heart of the book. I have interviewed hundreds of fathers with the intent to learn what active, effective dads do well. I have identified 13 contributions of fathers that I believe are unique and essential. A review of these contributions typically sparks contradictory responses from fathers and mothers. Fathers often report that my discussions of the contributions trigger memory-like reconnection of the roles universally attributed to fathers.

The contributions are:
- Financial Support
- Caregiving
- Trust
- Identity
- Family Traditions
- Security
- Self Protection
- Humor
- Courage
- Independence
- Self Confidence
- Patience
- Forgiveness

WHAT'S A MOTHER TO DO?

Mothers typically challenge the uniqueness of the contributions until they come to understand that men and women can offer the same contributions in very different ways. Because of the powerful relationships which mothers have with both fathers and children, successful fathering demands the cooperation and understanding of the mother. In this section, Gay Klinger, who is my wife, the mother of our son and my partner in our family therapy practice, joins me in discussion of each of the thirteen contributions. The purpose is to identify obstacles dads encounter as they attempt to become more active with their children and ways mothers can support the process of change.

ACCEPTING THE CHALLENGE

The goal of this last chunk is to help a father decide if he needs to make changes in his fathering, and if so, in which direction. I have provided a self scoring assessment tool along with tips about successful self change efforts.

Mothers typically challenge the uniqueness of the contributions until they come to understand that men and women can offer the same contributions in very different ways

1
Who *needs a* DAD *anyway?*

Who Needs a Dad Anyway?

WHO NEEDS A DAD, ANYWAY?

Have you ever thought about all the things you believe in? We say things like, "I believe in 'fair play'" or "I believe in God" or "all politicians are crooks." You may have never thought of it this way, but our beliefs—the things we believe in—direct the pathways of our lives. Not all of our beliefs can be reduced to simple statements. Many are complex and deeply rooted within the framework in which we view and understand reality. But our beliefs can be powerful influences over our lives. Beliefs are like computer programs that reflect our view of reality and influence our behaviors. For example, if we believe walking under a ladder is bad luck, we avoid such situations. If we believe friends are important, we are likely to seek them out. Some beliefs are shared by almost everyone in our society, such as the belief that children need to be cared for and protected.

What you may not have thought about is that beliefs, even those shared by our whole society, can change over time. They change as a result of other changes in our world that we may not be completely aware of at first but that become increasingly obvious over time.

Some changes in our beliefs may be positive and help us live better lives. An important example is the changing beliefs that Americans hold about smoking cigarettes. Fifty years ago, people in our country thought that cigarette smoking was harmless and a great way to relax. Now, most of us believe that smoking is a risk to our well-being.

Many in our society hold a belief about fathers. Specifically, there are those people whose belief about fathers can be summed up by the question... "Who needs a dad anyway?"

Whether you know it or not, over the past 30 years fathers have been disappearing from American families. Divorce has dramatically altered

Over the past 30 years fathers have been disappearing from American families.

the roles of fathers for nearly half the children in our country. Further, the cost of making a living and maintaining a family has resulted in both mom and dad working. Parents today spend 40% less time with their children than parents of the previous generation. Many of today's fathers have two or even three jobs. Other fathers travel weekly, taking them away from their families. In addition, alcoholism has taken a huge toll on the capability of some men to be fathers at all.

Each decade in the past 30 years has seen fewer fathers remaining in the home, working and playing active roles in the lives of their children. Let's consider how thirty years of progressively vanishing fathers has influenced our beliefs about fathering.

Many in our country no longer believe that children need fathers at all, except of course, to provide income. Our court systems and divorce laws reflect this view. It is also reflected in the belief that women claim owner-ship of babies at birth. In some cases, married couples have decided that if mom stays home to care for children, then it's a good idea for dad to devote himself full time to his career. In other situations, young men no longer equate their role in producing children born out of wedlock with fathering. Finally, the number of unwed women giving birth to children is staggering. The belief that fathers are not required is, in many cases, at the root of these situations.

Even strongly held beliefs may be incorrect at times. There is a flood of evidence that indicates that when fathers are absent their children are at risk. I will give you a concrete example that reflects the beliefs of American teenagers. Recently reported results of a survey showed that three out of four (75%) of today's teens believe that a single parent (i.e., single mother, since roughly 90% of single parents are female) can raise a family. Now let me give you the flip side of this issue.

While 75% of teenagers believe single mothers will do all right, the American Association of Retired Persons presents a more convincing view of the way things really are. The AARP reports that 3.4 million young children are being raised by their grandparents because their single moth-ers were unable to manage on their own. This is an increase of 40% over the past decade (AARP, 1996).

This book focuses on exploring the essential roles played by fathers in preparing their children for life as adults. Because many young male and female parents of today may have had absentee dads, they are confused about why dads are important and what they do. Since dad's role is linked to preparing children for adulthood, it is important for us to begin by looking at the demands of "the real world" or "real life."

WELCOME TO THE NFL! OR WHAT IS THE "REAL WORLD" REALLY LIKE?

I am not the first psychologist to come to the conclusion that most of the emotional problems we experience in life are caused by two things. Our unrelenting denial of the way life really is, and our exhausting attempts to deal with the bitter disappointment that results when we are disillusioned. For just a minute think about the way all of us talk about "the real world" or "real life" as if it is completely different from the way we would like to imagine the world to be. The clash between the way things really are and our fantasies about life frightens and distresses us.

What is really interesting about all this is how we adults not only fight to sustain our illusions, but to pass them on to our kids. I will give you an example. The world outside your family can be dangerous. A few years ago, in the typical middle class neighborhood where I work, a teenage boy decided one morning that he would like to experience how it really felt to shoot someone. So he started out on his adventure by picking a house, more or less at random. He rang the doorbell, managed to talk his way into the house and murdered two children while their mother showered down the hall.

The world outside your family can be dangerous.

The young killer was quickly found and gave himself up to the police. The neighborhood schools responded to the community's shock and grief by hosting family meetings and grief counseling sessions at the middle and elementary schools were the dead girl and boy had been students. I met with parents and students at both schools and my experiences there left a lasting impression.

At the middle school, toward the end of an evening session, a parent asked me if there were lessons they could take away from such a senseless and horrid event. We talked of several things, but the parents responded most eagerly to concrete suggestions about ways to prepare their children when encountering strangers wanting access to their homes. Common sense stuff really, but essential nevertheless.

With the receptive responses to my suggestions by the middle school parents in mind, I met the next morning with a group of parents at the elementary school the slain boy had attended. Having dealt with grief issues, I took the initiative and began talking about ways to protect young children by properly preparing them. Essentially, these were the same suggestions I had made to the middle school parents only modified to accommodate for the age differences. These parents, mostly mothers, did not like my suggestions in the slightest!

My suggestions were challenged on the grounds that they would destroy their children's sense of innocence. Preparing the children clearly meant acknowledging that danger existed, and that notion was too frightening for children to know about. Somehow, parenting had become equated with the conservation of innocence. Faced with the undeniable fact that every child in the school already knew that one of their classmates had been shot to death, the parents still chose denial as the best way to protect their children.

In his best selling book, *The Road Less Traveled*, M. Scott Peck begins his first chapter by stating, "Life is difficult....This is a great truth, one of the greatest truths." Actually, Dr. Peck was paraphrasing Buddha who taught that, "Life is suffering." My personal belief is that life is tough; very tough. It always has been, and it is not getting any easier.

Life is tough; very tough. It always has been, and it isn't getting any easier.

In the mid 1970's, a friend of mine earned a doctorate degree in Leisure Studies. Leisure Studies? For those of you who were not around, a myth of the '70's, which many experts endorsed completely, was that in the future the greatest problems to be faced by most Americans would be what we would do with our over abundance of leisure hours.

Recent evidence indicates that in the 1990's, not only do both mothers and fathers work at wage earning jobs, but that we are working more than ever before. American parents today, by some estimates, spend more time at work and less time with their children than did their parents. Wage earning has become a national obsession.

American parents spend 40% less time with their children than did their parents.

Wage earning. The most typical response that men give when asked to name their greatest contribution to their kids is earning a living. At the same time, when asked to pinpoint the greatest obstacle to being an active Dad, most men give the same answer. That's right...wage earning. Real life is a lot like work!

There are opportunities in the real world, but they are gained through hard work. The real world is competitive. There is no free lunch and at times, the rules of fair play simply do not exist. Unlike the love and understanding that parents give their kids inside the family, life at times is cold and uncaring.

And there is a lack of structure in the real world. Life demands that each of us define our own roles and dreams. We have to carve our own path; we have to know what it is we want to do and how to do it. In real life, if we wait around for others to tell us what we should do, chances are we are going to end up being manipulated. And speaking of manipulation, in real life trust carries the potential for betrayal. If we are too trusting or if we are careless about whom we trust, we are asking for betrayal.

The real world is characterized by continuous change, and we must adapt—like it or not.

Unlike our families, the real world or real life may seem uncaring and at times even cruel. One thing is certain however, it is not going to change to suit our preferences. To be successful, we must be prepared and we must be disciplined. As M. Scott Peck said, "Discipline is the basic set of tools we require to solve life's problems."

WHAT DOES IT TAKE TO BE SUCCESSFUL?

What do you think it takes to be successful in the real world? What does a person, male or female, need to know to be successful? Success in the real world demands that we have to be educated; we have to be skilled. We must demonstrate the competence to perform as a productive member of society. We must have the resiliency to deal with adversity.

We have to be goal-oriented. We cannot wander around hoping for the best. Therefore, we need the self-awareness to know what we really want. If we are to attain our goals we should know how to create opportunities on our own.

We have to be able to set our own priorities. I tell my son: if something is important, then treat it with importance. We cannot put the most important tasks at the bottom of the list.

We have to be tenacious; we have to be able to persevere. We have to know the ropes, work hard and be self-protective, not needy. We cannot go around begging for things we want or need. We have to be flexible and have the ability to adjust to change

We have to have a sense of values. Values provide a framework that directs and gives a sense of purpose to our lives. We have to know how to form alliances, deal with anxiety, absorb disappointment, be courageous and be independent.

As children grow and mature into adulthood, they must become self-reliant because Mom and Dad will not always be around to help them.

These are all valid points, and they effectively are the responses I have received during interviews with hundreds of men and women.

Most importantly, all the things I have listed here must be learned. This means that life skills must be taught, just as children go to school to learn math and reading. And it is our job as parents to teach life skills to our children.

Think about what we have just discussed. Think about what the real world is like and think about what our children are going to need to be capable of to be successful in real life.

THE FAMILY PROVIDES...

Now think about human children. What do we already know about children? Children need care, nurturing, protection and time to develop.

Human children grow to physical adulthood very slowly compared to other mammals. Furthermore, their brains, which develop very rapidly, do not come automatically "wired" for survival at an early age. Compare human children, say, with young wolves, bears or whales; and it's easy to see that we humans take a lot of time to grow and to learn to care for ourselves. Where does all this growing take place? That's right; it takes place in the family.

Our children do not come automatically "wired" for survival.

Think about families. Families have a major purpose. During my interviews and seminars, when I have asked for the words people associate with the word "family" they frequently come up with similar lists containing the following:

- Safety
- Security
- Caring
- Concern
- Forgiveness
- Predictability
- Stability
- Life Lessons

- Cooperation
- Dependency Tolerated
- Fairness; Rules
- Nurture
- Trust
- Acceptance with Nothing to Prove
- Emphasis on Relationship

Yes, families provide kids with all these things.

Think of your own family. Families provide safety, security, caring and comfort. These functions that families provide are extremely important to children. Let me repeat; human children are not able to go into the real world without support, direction and protection. They are unprepared to make it in the outside world. They grow up slowly and it is the parents' job to provide for their needs.

Over the years it has become more difficult for families to do the essential things let alone prepare kids for life. However, most families do a pretty good job of caring and providing security for their children. But, make no mistake. These things are necessary but not sufficient. It's important that we bring up our children in a safe, loving and nurturing environment. However, it is also our obligation to prepare them for life outside the comfort and security of the family. Real life demands more of parents. It demands that they both protect and prepare!

WHAT DOES MOM PROVIDE?

It is difficult to think about families without thinking about the contribution of mothers.

Everyone knows that mothers play major roles in child-rearing. During the past 30 years, while fathers were doing a disappearing act, mothers were on the job. So let's explore the contributions that mothers make within families.

Think about your mother or grandmother. What are words that come to mind which describe the contributions mothers make in the lives of children? Try the following, which are frequently offered during seminars:

- Rules/Limits
- Safety
- Nurture
- Support
- Care
- Comfort
- Sharing
- Rescue
- Protection
- Counseling/Relationships
- Avoidance of Danger
- Advice/Solve Problems
- Sustenance of Family
- Leveling
- Selflessness

A mother's primary concern is the safety and security of her children. Moms are quick to protect their children from threats. Mothers emphasize family relationships, sharing, nurturing and giving. Even career-minded working mothers acknowledge the primary importance of caregiving when describing their role with children. Through caregiving mothers express their love and assume the powerful role of teacher in the child's early life. Mothers associate caregiving with doing things, often everything, for the child. As a result, the child grows rapidly to trust and depend upon the mother.

A mother's primary concern is the safety and security of her children.

Let's think about the role of mother as teacher. How do you think mothers teach their children? That's right. They spend time with their children and establish rules. Mothers are "rule setters." Mother's rules are aimed at insuring their children's safety and that they are more or less socialized beasts. When rules are broken, Mom's anger, and the implied threat to the dependent relationship between child and mother, teaches

21

the child to behave.

I want to elaborate about the roles of mothers as rule setters. Moms make rules about nearly everything their kids do. Within most families there are two to three thousand rules that moms impose to control their youngsters' behaviors. And that's just before they start school.

Picture a typical mother as she says sweetly to the children: "Brush your teeth." "Chew with your mouth shut." "Go comb your hair!" and, "No, you cannot wear your underwear outside your clothes!" I don't really have a problem with the role of moms as rule setters. These rules act as powerful lessons and are linked to the mother's concern for their children's well-being.

So, if moms are rule setters, dads often find themselves as rule enforcers. Moms typically do not enforce their rules in the same way as fathers. Mothers become angry when rules are broken. Their anger threatens the mother-child relationship. Fathers seem less concerned with relationships and more with stopping misbehavior. Fathers combine anger with action. They tend to punish more often and with less conversation.

WHAT DOES DAD PROVIDE?

Now let's switch the focus to fathers. Think of your own dad, grandfather or uncles. What do you think about when you picture your dad or grandfather?

Discipline? Mom set the rules and dad enforced them. Teacher? How did dad teach? By example! That's right, role modeling.

An important point: *It is not what Dad says; it's what Dad does.* Keep that in mind. Kids remember only about 20% of what dads tell them, but *It is not what dad says; it's what dad does* they always remember what dads do. Kids are extremely observant of what dads do; a lot more than what dads say.

What are some of the things you remember about your dad, or know about yourself? Fun? OK, dads teach very often by playing with their kids. Play is crucial to effective fathering.

These are the things that the individuals I interviewed listed as typical of dads:

- Emphasize Skill; May be Critical
- Play Rough
- Discipline
- Impatient with Anxiety
- Play Hurt
- Work
- Don't Have to Like It
- Competitive
- Prepare for Life
- Set Limits

22

Dads emphasize the importance of skills development. In that role, they may be critical of their kids. They emphasize discipline. They are impatient when their kids are frightened. They tend to urge their kids to stretch themselves, to move into situations that may provoke anxiety. By example they often teach their children to be courageous, to work hard, to play sometimes even when hurt and that obligations override whether or not a person is tired or uncomfortable.

> *On Labor Day weekend I was working with my son, stripping rotten boards off my mom's deck. About halfway through — it was hot and about 100% humidity — we were both soaking wet, and we were covered with dirt.*
>
> *My son is twelve; his name is Christopher. He said, "Are we about ready to wrap this up?"*
>
> *And I said, "Christopher, all we've done is strip the boards off. If your grandmother walks out the door, there's about a 4 foot drop to the earth. No, we're not through. We're going to continue until we run out of boards. Or until we have this thing put back on."*
>
> *He said, "You know, I don't really like this."*
>
> *And I said, "Look, sport, I work in an air conditioned office. I don't like it any more than you do. I mean the truth of the matter is you don't have to like it. We're obligated. Your grandmother is our family and needs us to help her. She's on a fixed income. She can't pay to have this done. We're going to do it; we're going to finish this job. We're going to be here until it's done." And we did finish. Late that same evening my mom made dinner for the three of us and we all ate on her new porch.*

This is a contribution of fathering. Effective fathers teach that there are times when obligations override what we like or dislike.

WHAT DOES THE FAMILY PROVIDE?

Let's take a look at the family in terms of what both moms and dads provide.

Effective fathers teach that there are times when obligations override what we like or dislike.

What Does the Family Provide?

MOM	DAD
Rules/Limits	Discipline
Nurture	Play Rough
Support	Work
Care	Play Hurt
Comfort	Impatient with Anxiety
Sharing	Emphasize Skill; May be Critical
Rescue	Don't Have to Like It
Avoidance of Danger	Orient Toward Winning
Sustenance of Family	Have Boundaries
Leveling	Prepare for Life
Selflessness	
Counceling/Relationships	

Protection Preparation

These are the things a family provides. We can see that by working together, Mom and Dad provide safety and protection, as well as critical skills needed for life preparation.

Notice that there are things that moms and dads do together, and some that dads alone can offer. Notice, however, dad must be at home to do them.

Powerful evidence indicates that in America right now, the average amount of time that Dad spends with his youngsters, grades 1 through 6, is about 30 minutes a day. In those instances in which dads do spend time, it's only about an hour a day. How can dads teach their kids through role modeling if dads are never with their kids?

When Fathers Are Not Around

What happens is that Dad's role shifts to Mom. Most moms attempt to do what dads have done in past generations.

The evidence we have is that fathers are spending less time with their kids than did fathers a generation before. The time dads spend away from *Even the* their children is enough to create a gigantic gap in the skills that our kids *best of* need to take with them into the real world. Even the best of moms cannot *moms can-* be substitute dads. *not be sub-*

stitute dads. The issue is not that moms and dads are incapable of sharing roles. Fathers can learn much from their wives. The roles of fathers, however, are complementary to those mothers. They are unique and irreplaceable. A father's perspectives on life, personal ambition, discipline and skill development are typically not the same as the mother's. When a father is absent, a mother must be caregiver and protector, the usual role of a mother, while also encouraging the child to take risks and be self-reliant, the usual role of a father. The roles are often incompatible.

THE ROLE OF MOM AND DAD

Let's look at what we know.

We know that life in the real world is challenging for both men and women. We know that the role of the family is to protect and prepare children. We know that when asked people typically associate moms and dads with unique but complementary roles: moms with caregiving and dads with representing the outside world. We often see mothers as rule setters and that dads teach primarily by example or role modeling.

The Traditional View of the Role of Mom and Dad

Tasks Overlap, but all are essential.

MOM	DAD
Caregiving Inside the Family	Representative of the
Affiliation	World Outside the Family
How? Rule Setting	Autonomy
	How? Role Modeling

So where is the confusion? What is wrong with this traditional picture?

The roles of moms and dads are changing. More moms work. They are cops, career women and school teachers. Many dads spend a great deal of time with their children while mom is at work.

Depending on the family, there can be considerable overlap between the roles moms and dads play in families. There can also be considerable confusion! Newspapers and magazines tell us that the old division between moms' and dads' roles is a thing of the past! Things are more complex.

Many women attempt to resolve confusion by becoming both mom and dad for their children. Other women decide that the confusion and bother are so great that they will go it on their own without husbands.

Men, being men, tend to avoid situations when issues are complex and when they feel confused or incompetent. Some men say, "Maybe women are stronger than men, considering the nature of childbirth." Others have said, "Let her raise the kid. She's the mother. She's the one who wanted it!"

Clearly, the roles of mothers and fathers overlap. However, let's not be confused about the demands of child rearing. Women and men do not view life's challenges from the same perspective. The lessons taught by single men who are raising their children tell us that even when the tasks are the same, men and women place a different emphasis on how they do their jobs!

Men play more roughly with both boy and girl children than do women. They place a greater emphasis on competition and winning while women place greater value on cooperation and playing just for fun. Though mothers and fathers share concern for their child's safety, men tend to spend time teaching their child how to protect themselves while mothers typically admonish children to avoid threatening situations.

Children have a greater chance of being successful in the world outside the security of family when both mom and dad have played their roles...

While neither perspective is more or less legitimate than the other, they are very different!

Children have a greater chance of being successful outside the comfort and security of family when both mom and dad have played their roles, regardless of how great or little they overlap. Mothers, through rule setting, are powerful teachers and children need them. Fathers portray through their day-to-day interactions with the children, mother and others that the responsibilities and obligations of fathers are no less essential.

Each decade more fathers drift away from their children. In many instances they seem not to realize they even have a parenting role. Others feel confused about how to be a father. One thing is certain; as fathers have disappeared, families have become "unbalanced."

We may not like to admit it, but we are fast moving toward a society in which the young men and women to whom we once confidently pointed as tomorrow's leaders are unprepared to live as independent adults. I have a variety of ways to support that statement. For example, there is a subpopulation known as the "boomerang generation". These are young adults who attempt to leave home, fail, then come back to live with their mothers and fathers.

I've been a psychologist for years, and increasingly I work with people in their late fifties and sixties who ask, "What are we supposed to do? My grownup son just moved back home," or "my daughter just came home with three kids."

For many of these older parents it is too late to go back and relive their lives as a way of correcting past mistakes. But most readily admit that they failed to prepare their now adult children for real life. In many of these instances the father was missing from the parenting equation. Our children must be prepared to live when we are no longer able to provide for them. This job takes both a mother and a father.

CHILDREN NEED THE BALANCE

Children need the balance of a mother and a father.

Children need the balance of a mother and a father.

Over the past three decades, mothers have been there. Mothers have been on the job. Even working mothers attempt to fill their role within the family.

Regrettably, many fathers have come to believe that their job relates exclusively to wage earning. However, the lesson taught by effective fathers is that the obligations of fathers extend beyond wage earning.

WHEN DAD IS ACTIVE

When dads are actively involved with their children the results are irreversible!

When dads are active:

- School performance is higher; children are less likely to fail grades and are more likely to graduate. A recent study demonstrated that when dads are involved with their kids, SAT and grade levels are 38% higher than when dads are not involved.
- In terms of behavior, youngsters without an active dad, regardless of economic level or race, are four times more likely to get in trouble in school than when dad is involved.
- In terms of self-esteem and self-protection, children are less likely to experience anxiety disorders or to be socially avoidant when they have an active dad.
- Greater ambition, respect for the opposite sex, and stronger sexual identity are also characteristics of children who have active fathers.
- When dads involve themselves in the family, children are more

resilient and male children have more respect for women because they see their father being respectful toward their mother. Female children are more ambitious. Eighty-five percent of the young women enrolled in college have active fathers.

ACTIVE DADS

It's been my experience in interviewing successful dads that the roles of moms and dads are not the same; the orientation of men is not the same as women. The attitudes, the experiences, the traditions and the priorities of men are not the same as those of women.

Men contribute uniquely to the lives of their children.

Both parents care for their children. They both want the best for their children.

I have discovered that men contribute uniquely to the lives of their children.

Think about the types of things active dads do with their children. Look over these Do's and Don'ts:

Do's	Don'ts
Play, hold, read, talk	Leave job to Mom
Help with homework	Work all the time
Come home, take kids with you	Assume Mom knows best
Rethink priorities	Leave school, doctor, "taxi
Consider the essential nature	driving" to Mom
of your role	Bury self in TV, bottle, computer

In the chapters to come we are going to talk about the characteristics of active dads in ways that more precisely define what successful fathers do that work.

MEN ARE NOT WOMEN, AND FATHERS ARE NOT MOTHERS

Fathers cannot be replaced.

Dad's role is complementary to that of Mom and it's irreplaceable. The evidence is overwhelming. We know for certain that attempting to raise children without fathers is not working.

In a certain sense, the Murphy Brown ideal—the idea that a woman can raise a child successfully without a father—is a myth. Only about four percent of the women in our society have the financial capability to bring up a child with a adequate standard of living.

Those single mothers who are financially capable, in many instances, find that by the time the child reaches middle school age, problems arise in their behavior and school progress. We will be talking more about the issues in the next section.

Recently I saw a T-shirt on display in a window of a women's bookstore. The T-shirt had a message printed on its front. It read, "A woman needs a man like a fish needs a bicycle." You know, the message might be true. Women may not need men, but children need fathers.

...a woman may not need a man, but a child needs a father.

Fathers need not be perfect. I have talked with hundreds of hardworking, devoted fathers who readily admit that they are not always models of perfection. These fathers share, however, a grasp of the importance of the role that they play with their children, as well as the sense that fathering is not the same as mothering. What I have come to believe is that flawed, yet active, fathers are genuine representatives of the real world. In an upcoming section we will look at the contributions of fathers and you can decide for yourself how you are doing. It's my guess that most of you will find that you are on the right track. But some of you may need to rethink your priorities.

Before we talk about the positive aspects of fathering though, we need to face up to a darker side of fathering...the consequences of absent dads.

2

Absent DADS/

Lost Kids

Absent Dads/Lost Kids

The author is especially appreciative of Wade F. Horn, Ph.D. and the staff of the National Fatherhood Initiative who collected and published much of the information presented in this section.

ABSENT DADS/LOST KIDS

I f we look closely at the status of fathering, we see a coin with two sides. On one side of the coin is the good news about fathering. On the other is the bad news. Right now we are going to look at the bad news; and there is much bad news to talk about. Fathering is in a state of crisis in our country and our children's futures are at risk.

Fathering is in a state of crisis and our children's futures are at risk.

Many of the issues that we will explore will not be much fun to think about. It's necessary, however, because experience has taught us that when negative changes occur slowly, we humans typically attempt to pretend that nothing is really wrong or that what is happening to others will never influence us personally.

As we have discussed, over the past 30 years fathers have been vanishing from American families. According to the U.S. Bureau of Census, "50% of all white children and 75 % of all African-American children will live some portion of their childhood without their fathers." No other country in the world has a greater percentage of fatherless families. Alarmingly, nearly 27% of all the children in our country are born into single parent homes.

As a consequence we Americans are becoming unjustifiably confident that fatherless families are no different from those with dads. There is reason for major concern about fatherlessness and this is our focus as we explore Absent Dads & Lost Kids.

WHO ARE ABSENTEE DADS?

Fatherless families. Single parent, female head of household families. Vanishing fathers. Disappearing dads. What is going on here? Was it ever any different? What difference does it make anyway?

Who are Absentee Dads?

Let's take the time to get a better understanding of absentee dads, as well as the consequences of fatherlessness. We will start with some basics. Where do you think the term absentee dad comes from?

Exactly, at its most fundamental level, "absentee dads" are men who are the biological fathers of children with whom they do not live! The dads and children live apart. There are at least two major types of dads who live apart from their children. Who would you guess represents the greatest number of absentee dads in America? Yes, that's right...divorced men.

Everyone already knows that we Americans have the highest divorce rate in the world (approximately 50% of first marriages fail). It's amazing how commonly accepted this figure has become.

About 90% of non-custodial parents are fathers.

See how this sounds. Since 1960, the number of children involved in divorce has leaped from 463,000 (1960) to about one million (1990). The number of children living only with their mother jumped from 5.1 million in 1960 to 15.6 million kids by 1993! That's right, and according to experts about 90% of non-custodial parents are fathers.

Think of the impact on a child's life when the father is removed from the family. Tell me this, how are kids to learn from someone to whom they have only limited access? The answer is grim.

In families disrupted by divorce only one child in six has seen the father as often as once a week. That's only 17%! About 40% of children whose parents are divorced have not seen their father in at least a year. It gets worse. Ten years after divorce, more than two-thirds of kids living with their mother report not seeing their father for a year. More than 50% of kids living in fatherless homes have never spent the night in their dad's home. More than 25% of absent dads live in another state. Anybody can see that for most kids divorce brings a dramatic reduction in interaction between father and child.

Non-custodial fathers become more like relatives than fathers.

What about non-custodial fathers who attempt to stay in touch with their children? Ask yourself — how do you think relationships change if a child who once saw both of their parents seven days a week, began seeing one of them on Wednesdays and every other weekend? The relationship changes dramatically.

As years pass, non-custodial fathers become more like relatives than fathers. Divorced fathers become "Uncle Dad." Non-custodial dads are disconnected from the day-to-day experiences of their children's lives. Like it or not these dads often evolve into "treat Dads," whose time with kids is spent going to movies, vacations and special events. Lost are opportunities to work with children at homework, share life experiences or provide guidance and discipline.

*Non-custo-
dial fathers
become
more like
relatives
than fathers.*

INVISIBLE FATHERS

Now let's shift our attention to perhaps the fastest growing sub-population of absentee fathers. Any guess about who these absent dads might be?

If you thought about unmarried (and non-custodial) fathers, you were correct. How important is this issue? Well, each year more than one million babies in our country are born to unwed women. Is this more than in past decades? I guess! In 1960, less than ten percent of all children were born to unwed mothers. At present, almost 30% are born out of wedlock. Fifty % of unwed mothers are among the lowest income households in our country. Currently, 81% of teenagers who give birth are unmarried (this is up from 33% in the 1960's).

So, what is the role of unmarried, non-custodial fathers? These are the invisible fathers. In truth, we know little about these fathers apart from the negative information provided by child support authorities (for example, only 44.5% are current with child support payments). The obstacles they face appear enormous. While 57% of fathers whose kids are younger than two years of age visit their child more than once weekly, by the time the child has turned two 1/2 years old this percentage begins dropping to about 23% maintaining frequent contact.

Most disturbing, a recognized expert who has devoted his career to working with teenage fathers, reports that few teenage males equate sexual interaction with fathering. There are equally powerful indications that unwed mothers (and their family members) actively work to keep the child's father out of the child's life, except for financial support.

If our beliefs really do act like computer programs that direct the ways we believe, then we have to change the thinking of our country's teenagers! Teenage girls are not successful at raising children on their own. They depend upon others such as their parents and welfare to support them and their children.

When they begin to grow up, their children are more likely to live in poverty, get minimal medical care and do poorly in school. There is an overwhelming chance that their male children will turn to drugs, gang related activity and crime. Their female children will become unwed teenage mothers themselves. We have to get this message into the public schools without delay.

FAMILY VERSUS CAREER

There is a final group of absent dads that you may not have considered. Here is a hint. They are not divorced, but in many ways they live apart from their children. Who are these guys?

Let's spend a little time with this one. In this decade the inescapable fact has hit home that financially maintaining a family requires a very high commitment of time and energy to earn money. Living is extremely costly. As a consequence mothers and fathers often work. As I mentioned today's parents spend about 40% less time with their children than did parents of earlier generations. Now that's a significant time deficit! Over one and one half million children (ages 5 to 14 years) return from school to an empty home.

Increasingly women in our society work outside the home and are mothers at the same time. However, we still view fathers as the primary source of income (and they do contribute, on average, about 70% of the family financial support). In some cases married couples decide that it is a good idea for dad to devote his full attention to earning money or advancing his career and thereby allow mom to focus on child rearing. As a consequence, more than 75% of our children in two parent homes grow up without a significant father-child interaction.

Estimates are that fewer than 25% of our young children spend at least one hour daily with their fathers. The average amount of even relatively individualized time dads spend with their children is less than 30 minutes. As kids grow older (that is 6th through 12th grades), the amount of time drops. Only 20% of fathers and children report having a ten minute conversation at least once a month.

Like divorced dads, the always-at-work fathers often adopt the "quality time" mind set. They become special event dads; "treat" dads.

Make no mistake, the father's contributions to his children go beyond financial support. From the child's perspective, a workaholic dad may remove the financial hardships faced by children of unwed parents, but provide few benefits not offered by divorced non-custodial fathers. Like divorced dads, the always-at-work fathers often adopt the "quality time" mind set to justify the hours they spend away from the family. In short, they become special event dads; "treat" dads. Their children are more familiar with their Game Boys than their fathers.

I have found little difference between dads who are separated from their kids by divorce and those who are preoccupied with work, except economically. They are both absentee fathers in my book. They are outside the lives of their children. Too often they equate fathering with being included in photo opportunities with their kids. Workaholic dads may nail down promotions and bonuses, but they fail the test of fatherhood. They abandon their children.

AWOL FATHERS

There are other absentee dads as well. There are those who are emotionally absent. Everyone knows the saying, "The lights are on, but nobody's home." Well, these guys fit comfortably under that umbrella.

They are drunks or drug users. They are dependent men incapable of modeling how adult males deal with the real world or life's problems because they run away.

They are TV or computer junkies. They disconnect from family life because it's too loud, too complex or too confusing.

They suffer from depression. Life is hard and some men have been wounded. These men wish only to be left alone.

Then there are boy-like men. They have adult bodies, but emotionally they are immature. They are selfish and self-centered. They do not just play soccer, cycle or golf. Their games are their top priority. They do not want to grow up. They do not want to be fathers or to have responsibilities.

There are also men who love their sons, but never notice their daughters. They will carry their sons around the world, but never give their daughter a thought. They are blind.

These men are MIAs; missing from their children's lives. Their children, more often than not, are "Lost Kids."

WHO ARE THE "LOST KIDS"?

We pretty well covered the bases when talking about Absent Dads, so let's turn our attention to the "Lost Kids." Our emphasis in this and upcoming discussions will be on how well kids without fathers are prepared to live in a competitive, demanding world.

Lost Kids! What images do those words trigger in your thinking?

Lost? Yes, without guidance, without support.

Children need a mother and a father. Those with only a single parent

The major benefit associated with being white in our society is usually that of being from a two-parent family.

are more likely to be lost. For one thing 55% of kids growing up in single parent families live in poverty. This means that health and medical requirements compete with other basic needs, such as food and shelter.

Researchers have determined that the major benefit associated with being white in our society is usually that of having a two-parent family. When this type of family is disrupted, the children involved become dramatically more likely to meet with problems in their lives.

Think of your own experiences. Everyone knows of families touched by divorce. Perhaps you have been personally. Think about the challenges faced by single parent families.

The children of disrupted families experience problems in many areas: educational, behavioral, emotional and, in some cases, criminal behavior. For example, the female children of single female parents are more likely to become unwed teenage mothers. We will discuss these issues in greater detail as we explore the consequences of fatherlessness in American families.

Without fathers most children lack the support, guidance and discipline required to deal with life outside the family and, in many instances, within it.

WHEN DO LOST KIDS GET "LOST"?

By now nearly everyone has thought of at least one exception to the problems attributed to absent dads. In the past, many have questioned the notion that children suffer without an active dad in the family. In particular single parents of young children often express disbelief that absent fathers are essential because few problems with their children are apparent.

Perhaps because young children require high levels of caregiving, problems may not emerge. Additionally, pre-schools and elementary schools are based primarily on caregiving models with great emphasis on structure, comfort, security and nurturing. As a consequence, the early years of a child's school life seem to replicate life within an extended family.

Adolescence is not about play. It is more like a dress rehearsal for life (as in "real life").

But consider the differences between elementary school and middle school. There are major differences. It is sometimes said that the work of childhood is play. Well, adolescence is not about play. It is more like a dress rehearsal for life (as in "real life"). Middle school teachers expect self-reliance. They expect students to behave, to act like young adults. Middle school is where lost children "become lost."

The competition for passing grades, sports teams, and peer acceptance is more intense. Those who cannot compete well are elbowed outward into the fringe groups. Without self discipline or support, these children experience failure, disappointment and frustration. Their self confidence is broken.

These experiences are common real life situations. Everyone must learn to deal with frustration and challenges to our comfort and security. Fatherless children do not deal well with such challenges.

So, the real answer is that kids can become "lost" at any time between birth and middle school. The appearance that they are "lost" usually occurs during the middle school years. However, this is just the phase of their life when they stand out and their problems become readily visible.

CONSEQUENCES OF FATHERLESS KIDS

Let's take a closer look at the consequences of fatherless children.

We will start by looking at criminal activity, educational problems and disciplinary problems. In this section there are a flood of statistics to keep up with, but I have provided them primarily to convey the magnitude of the relationship between absent dads and the types of problems their kids experience.

Juvenile delinquency

When fathers are absent from the home, adolescent and teenage boys are two to four times more likely to be arrested for juvenile offenses. So powerful is the relationship between fatherlessness and juvenile crime that this factor alone is more predictive than race, poverty level and educational level. The greatest predictor of juvenile crime is the presence or absence of a father in the home.

Juvenile crime is getting much worse. Arrest rates for violent crime, including murder, aggravated assault, forcible rape and car theft, rose dramatically between 1982 and 1991. In most cases these rates exceeded 90% increases. Now let's look at who was being arrested.

Of those juveniles sentenced to state reform institutions, 70% came from single or no parent backgrounds. This contrasts dramatically with the 13% of delinquents who came from families with both a mother and father living together. Seventy-two percent of adolescent murders and 60% of rapists grew up without fathers.

So powerful is the relationship between fatherlessness and juvenile crime that this factor alone is more predictive than race, poverty level and educational level.

Educational problems

In disrupted families, children report lower educational expectations by parents, and less monitoring and supervision of homework and other activities than children from two parent families. Children without fathers typically adopt friends who place low importance on working hard to make good grades.

As a result, about one third of students from disrupted families report a significant decline in academic performance, which can last up to three years. Children living in non-intact families are two times more likely to repeat a grade than students living with both parents. The dropout rate is also two times greater for fatherless children.

While only 17% of high achievers come from single parent homes, 38% of low achievers are fatherless. Eighty-five percent of students from intact, two parent families attend college.

Disciplinary problems

Boys who got in trouble for violent misbehavior while at school were 11 times more likely to come from father-less homes.

Once again, the behavior of fatherless boys is predictable. Boys who got in trouble for violent misbehavior while at school were 11 times more likely to come from fatherless homes. Nationally, the number of boys who were expelled from school was from two to four times greater when living with a never married or a divorced mother than children living with both parents.

Out-of-Wedlock childbearing

As we previously reported, teenage women who give birth are very likely to have total family incomes less than half of the poverty level income. Consider this: 79% of teenage, unmarried school dropouts live in poverty. Great expectations for the future, right?

Well, there are some predictable expectations. One expectation is that the male children of unmarried, poverty level mothers will get in trouble with the law, repeat grades and drop out of school. Another is that both male and female children born to unmarried mothers will be likely to bear out-of-wedlock children themselves. This expectation is especially strong for females.

Daughters of single mothers are 111% more likely to have children as teenagers; 164% more likely to have a premarital birth; 53% more likely to marry as teenagers and 92% more likely to dissolve these marriages.

Emotional problems

Fatherless children have more difficulty forming and maintaining peer relationships than those from two parent families. Female children from divorced families have higher rates of anxiety. Male children experience severe role identity problems.

Children are two to three times more likely to exhibit significant emotional problems when living apart from their biological fathers. Eighty percent of adolescents treated in psychiatric hospitals come from disrupted homes. Three of four teenage male suicide victims lived in female headed, single parent households.

Children living apart from their biological fathers may be 40 times more likely to be abused than are children of the same age living with both biological parents.

The problem is getting worse rapidly, and the consequences go further.

Consequences go further...

A consistent observation about fatherless kids is that they appear to have a need for acceptance by older males. This need takes the form of a yearning for male approval. This is sometimes portrayed by the adoption of styles of dress, attitudes, opinions and lifestyles of older males by young boys. Juvenile court authorities have a long standing understanding of powerful influence older teens and young adults play in recruiting adolescent boys into criminal activity.

In a similar fashion, while the age of teenage, unmarried mothers has dropped to an all-time low, unmarried fathers are most often above the age of twenty. Boy and girl children with physically or emotionally absent fathers often exhibit this "father hunger," or need for a positive connection with their missing father.

When fathers are unavailable, children turn to the most readily accessible source of masculine influence. At one time older brothers, uncles, grandfathers and trusted family friends may have filled the shoes of absentee dads. However, with the disruption of more and more families in our society, street gangs have increasingly replaced positive sources of male influence.

Many of today's kids turn to the mother as a source of information about their fathers. The mother's portrait of husbands and fathers presents, at best, a picture devoid of the actual feelings, attitudes, points of view, history and spontaneity of a genuine father-child relationship.

When fathers are unavailable children come to think of fathers primarily as ideas, not as real people.

Children come to think of fathers primarily as ideas, not as real people. As a consequence, boy and girl children attempt to avoid or emulate fathers outside their actual experience. It's much like Japanese citizens attempting to dress and adopt the singing styles of American Country and Western performers. It is just not the same as the real thing.

As a society we have attempted to respond to the absence of fathers by creating big brother/sister and mentoring programs in public schools. Despite these efforts, we are losing the battle. Kids without dads are more likely to use drugs, join gangs and end up in juvenile court. In past years, the Armed Forces may have served as training opportunities that introduced boys and girls into adulthood, but today's peacetime armies provide limited opportunity.

Perhaps of greatest concern is the cultural discounting of the role of fathers in our country. Within our nation's judicial system, in private businesses and within many families, fathers are viewed as unnecessary, troublesome and, at times, dangerous.

Many dads appear clueless about what fathering means in today's family.

Even worse, many dads appear clueless about what fathering means. Lacking adequate fathers of their own, they fail to view themselves as active contributors to the lives of their sons and daughters. As a result, future generations of males and females will enter their adult lives inadequately prepared and ill equipped to deal with adversity or opportunity.

WHAT SUSTAINS FATHERLESSNESS?

A major purpose of our discussion of these issues is to raise our awareness of the pervasiveness of fatherlessness and to dispel the notion that fathers play insignificant roles in their kids' lives. However, experience has taught that while awareness is necessary it is not sufficiently powerful by itself to turn the tide of fatherlessness in our country. My work with fathers, for example, revealed that many young fathers, while distressed to learn that they were inadequate dads, had not a clue about what to do differently!

I also discovered that there are factors that seem to sustain fatherlessness.

Even though a flood of evidence supports the notion that dads must be active with children, bringing dads back into the parenting equation may not be that easy. Let's focus on the myths and misconceptions that create obstacles to father-child interaction. Look these over.

DIVORCE

We could probably talk about divorce and custody issues forever. Everybody knows how painful the process of divorce is on adults and children. The adversarial nature of the divorce process creates a win-lose mentality that emphasizes the artificial segregation of roles, establishes unnatural models for visitation and sustains the notion that fathers play ambiguous and tangential parenting roles.

ECONOMICS

Life is extremely costly. Both men and women in our society devote increasingly larger portions of their lives to wage earning and less to their families. As adults attempt to solve the problems of achieving financial stability, it is often the father who works longer hours, takes on second ("moonlighting") jobs and thus spends less time with the family. In addition, many jobs require out of town travel that pulls parents, and especially fathers, outside the family loop.

MYTHS

Myths are stories or sayings that are not real, but everybody believes are true anyway! Many times we adopt certain myths without giving a second thought to whether they are true or false. We just assume things to be a certain way. Some myths sustain absentee dads. Here's the first:

Moms own children

Did you ever think about ownership of children? Sounds un-American, doesn't it? Nevertheless, many men and women believe that mothers own their children. Author Victoria Secunda in her book, *Women and Their Fathers*, states that at the moment of birth, many women seize psychological ownership of their children.

This belief is simply untrue. However, just imagine how it could influence the father's position in the parenting equation if either or both of the child's parents believe that the child belongs to the mother. Essentially the father is disenfranchised; he loses his vote. His opinions are automatically discounted.

Many men and women believe that mothers own their children.

41

Raising children is women's work

Nationally, we Americans share the myth that it is somehow not masculine to care for children. Yet, there is a rapidly growing number of single fathers who dispute this belief every day by working at their paid jobs and raising their children.

These men are dock workers, printers, engineers and meat cutters. They are from every race, religion and culture. Some have college degrees and others are working on their GEDs. They are men who work. But they are also men who have chosen to arrange their lives in such a way as to provide time for child rearing as well. They prove that masculinity and child rearing can go together.

Girls do not need fathers

Why don't girls need fathers? Tell me. Of course girls need mothers. They are the same sex. Yes, girls and moms have much in common. Why does that in any way negate the need of girls for their fathers? How would a girl benefit from involvement with her dad?

Briefly, girls with active and hardworking dads are more ambitious, more successful in school, attend college more often and attain careers of their own.

They are less dependent. They are more self-protective. Girls with active dads are less likely to date or marry abusive men. If they do become involved with an abusive male they can recognize their situation and get themselves out of the relationship.

Girls with active dads are less likely to get pregnant as teenagers. Few marry before they graduate from high school. When they do choose a mate, they are likely to choose a man who is hardworking and who will treat them with respect. Any questions?

MISCONCEPTIONS

Kids and adults actually think very much alike. All of us make observations and reach conclusions based on our experiences. From time to time, we arrive at conclusions that seem to make sense but are not entirely accurate. Some misconceptions concern fathering and, while they appear rational, sustain fatherlessness. Consider these:

My kids have a loving mom, I'll focus on my work and career

Currently, many parents in our society have decided that it is a sound parenting decision for dad to work as much as possible to enable mom to stay home with the children. The belief is that if kids have a loving, caring mother they can do without dad. While it is true that children benefit from stay-at-home moms, even the best of moms cannot be substitute fathers. Such families are out of balance and their children are at risk. Often these children experience the same type of problems as kids whose moms and dads are divorced.

Even the best of moms cannot be substitute dads.

Dad can step in when kids are older

Some fathers have decided that small children do not need Dad's influence. These men believe that the things grown men have to offer require more attention, strength, self control or whatever, than little kids can sustain. It's easy for a dad to tell himself that when the kids are about 12 years old, he will be able to step in and really have a positive influence. It's hard to know where to start with this cockeyed notion.

While it's true that 12-year-olds are good candidates for dads' attention, why wait until the kid is 12? My experience has taught me that 12-year-olds with absent dads are uncertain about their sense of competence. They have trouble staying focused and they avoid situations in which they might look bad.

Twelve-year-olds unfamiliar with father-child interactions may not trust their dad. They will probably resent his lack of previous involvement. Chances are very great that they will have become over-dependent on the mother and show little interest in dad's favored activities, opinions or suggestions.

Finally, 12-year-olds are beginning an important separation process from their parents. Typically, they are primarily interested in their peer relationships. A father attempting to step into the picture at this stage of their development may find himself competing for his child's attention with other kids who have a lot more in common with his child than he does.

I can make up for being gone ...

Where did the term "quality time" ever come from, anyway? It probably sounded like a great idea once, but I believe we are overdue to revise the

43

Quality time is seldom "special" time. Quality time happens in the day-to-day mundane activities of life.

current use of "quality time" as it applies to fathering. Many absentee dads excuse themselves from everyday involvement in their kids' lives by making scheduled appearances for these so-called "quality time" experiences. They show up for photo opportunities with their children.

The lessons taught by effective dads is that quality time is seldom "special" time. Quality play may involve roughhousing or play, but just as often it's holding a sick child. Quality time is doing homework, building school projects, or talking with a child who has been in an emotionally-charged school yard fight. Quality time sometimes means having arguments, setting limits or saying "no." Quality time happens in the day-to-day mundane activities of life. Remember, truly heroic dads are not viewed as heroes by their kids. They are not special, because they are always around.

DADS ARE ESSENTIAL

If we consider the magnitude of the negative consequences associated with fatherlessness, it is not difficult to agree that fathers are essential. Think about the word essential. Absolutely required. When something that is essential is missing, whatever might have been is no longer the same. For example, if we agree that chairs have four legs, what happens if we remove one of the legs? We can rebuild it as a stool. We can sit on it, but it is no longer a chair.

In the same way, dads are irreplaceable.

If they are absent, the family is not likely to work as well as a family with both parents. It's like a three-legged chair. We can still call it a family, but it is out of balance.

I repeat: Children need the balance of a mother and a father. We have tried to act out our belief that dads are replaceable but they are not. Today's world is complex and challenging. Relationships between men and women seem more difficult to maintain. Nevertheless, children still need two parents to protect and prepare them for life as adults.

Remember, effective dads do what absent dads are not around to do.

WHERE DO WE GO FROM HERE?

As we have seen, our society has been changing. Over the past three decades single parent families have dramatically replaced families with both parents. The percentage of babies born to unwed mothers has sky-rocketed. Fathers have moved outside the child rearing loop. And, the consequences of fatherless families are apparent.

Children need their fathers. That much is simple.

What appears necessary is determining what are the essential qualities provided by fathers.

Regrettably, much of what we know about fathering is negative. We hear about deadbeat dads, absentee dads, teenage dads, abusive dads, alcoholic dads and workaholic dads. So pervasive is the negative information about fathers, that many people have come to doubt that we can or even should halt the trend toward fatherlessness in our country. Some individuals seem to view fatherlessness as a plague that has swept across our country and is hopelessly irreversible.

Heroic dads are not viewed as heroes by their kids. They are not special, because they are always around.

There is a fathering crisis, but I have discovered that there are still heroic examples of fathers within our society. Fortunately, there is still a sizable group of competent fathers; however, their numbers are shrinking as ever decade passes. Over the past half decade, I have interviewed hundreds of men, women and children. From these individuals I have discovered the benefits of fathering. Further, my interviews have allowed me to collect and sort through the unique contributions fathers offer their children.

The contributions of effective dads provide direction for absentee dads yearning to return to an active role in the family. The lessons offer specific guidelines for young adults who are confused about the roles of fathers within today's complex family structures. For divorced dads, the contributions serve as powerful reminders that fathering obligations extend beyond financial support. Finally, these contributions provide competencies for teenage mothers and fathers to learn about and adopt as they evaluate their candidacy for parenthood.

So, in our next section we will explore these unique and irreplaceable "Contributions of Effective Fathers."

3

What's *a*

FATHER

to *Do?*

What's a Father To Do?

As a family psychologist, I have conducted countless parent training programs over the years. As with anything else, the more familiar I became with the material taught in these parenting classes, the more capable I was of paying attention to the reactions of the men and women attending them. I became aware that while both parents were concerned about their children, they had different interests. At times the mothers would seem very connected with the material. At other times, the men would become more involved, while their wives appeared less interested.

For example, a fair share of most parenting material is aimed at improving communication skills and building stronger relationships. In many instances, the mothers in class not only enthusiastically embraced these notions, but made attempts to insure that their husbands were paying attention (as often as not, the dads were heaving heavy sighs and looking at their watches).

I noticed, however, that when the topics addressed children's behavior, the dads seemed to wake up and pay more attention. It's not unusual, for instance, for parenting classes to present approaches to child discipline that emphasize the use of logical or natural consequences to increase children's appropriate behavior and decrease inappropriate behaviors. The lessons are very straight forward. If the child does as instructed, positive things happen. If the child fails to comply, negative things follow. Nine times out of ten, the dads loved it. Many mothers, however, viewed such approaches with discomfort and were reluctant to set up or consistently follow through with them.

Their resistance stemmed from the imagined threat that using logical or natural consequences might have on their relationship with their children. That is, specifying appropriate versus inappropriate behaviors, and prearranging positive and negative consequences threatened the very core of the mother-child relationship. Is this because the child, given the choice to earn positive or negative outcomes, becomes more independent? If so, can it be that the child's independence may threaten some mothers? These and other father-mother differences became apparent to me.

The child's independence may threaten some mothers.

For example, when I first accepted the invitation to start a fathers' "support group" at an elementary school near my office, I already knew that "fathering" did not necessarily carry the same meaning as "mothering." I was uncertain, however, of exactly how the roles of mothers and fathers differed or perhaps overlapped, so I decided to use the fathering group as a vehicle to explore these issues.

My initial efforts were frustrating for everyone. I discovered that the men who showed up for the "support" group were not particularly eager to share their inadequacies as fathers with other men. As John Gray, Ph.D. discussed in *Men are from Mars, Women are from Venus,* my experience verified that men typically avoid situations in which they may appear incompetent. Instead, men view support as concrete information from a recognized expert. And I was supposed to be the expert!

Luckily, I previously had learned that most people enjoy being interviewed. Most of us enjoy telling other people our ideas, opinions and experiences if given an opportunity. I explained, in a very authoritative manner, that to organize the material for the upcoming sections, I needed to interview them. Although they agreed to play along, my initial efforts landed face down once again. When asked directly to describe the unique roles of fathers, I discovered something that I had not predicted but which later interviews verified in the years to come. What I found was that most young fathers had few clear ideas, besides wage earning, of what they offer to their children. Their silence was embarrassing testimony to the status of fathers in today's families.

This book is a tribute to the perseverance of those men who continued to return to my first "ragtag" efforts at working with fathers. Eventually, I was successful at untapping the information I had hoped was there all along. By requesting that each individual focus on the roles played by mothers, I found the key. Everybody knows what moms do.

Moms love, care, listen, feed and protect. Moms will not let you kill your little brother or let your older sister cheat. They get angry and they have rules for nearly every situation. Over the past half decade, I have asked the same question and the responses are always the same.

What I found interesting was that, having listed the things moms do, most participants find it easier to talk about what dads, grandfathers, uncles, older brothers or somebody else's dads do. As one participant put it, "A dad is where you find him, even if he is your older cousin." Slowly, the portrait of fathers began to emerge and with it the contributions that children need from their father.

"A dad is where you find him, even if he is your older cousin."

Based on my interviews with over 1000 men, I have identified 13 contributions that fathers give to their children. Presented here are the "Contributions of Fathers":

- Financial Support
- Caregiving
- Trust
- Identity
- Family Traditions
- Security
- Self Protection
- Humor
- Courage
- Independence
- Self Confidence
- Patience
- Forgiveness

As you will discover, the contributions of mothers and fathers overlap. Yet, it is my belief that men and women do not parent in the same way. Further, it is my finding that while it might be possible for a mother to act as both mom and dad, in most instances they do not.

The focus on the fathers' role has become necessary primarily because children best learn about fathering from their father. Across the decades, women have maintained the connection between themselves and their children. Regrettably, it is we men who have become disconnected from our roles as fathers. The contributions of fathers presented here is an attempt not to criticize mothers, but to help today's fathers be the best they can be.

Children best learn about fathering from their father.

As you might imagine, not even the best of fathers will claim to do an outstanding job in all the areas I have identified. My attempt has not been to create the profile of an ideal father. Instead, it's been my intent to provide bench marks for fathers, against which to measure themselves as dads. Further, these guidelines can be used by mothers to determine missing puzzle parts in the family structure. Remember, awareness is just the first step to constructive change. Acknowledgment is the second and acceptance is the most critical.

Take a minute to look back over the contributions of fathers. Chances are, many of you are already doing a good job on most of these contributions. In some instances, however, you may discover that there are areas in which you could improve. Later, you will have the opportunity to assess yourself against these contributions and possibly you may decide to modify the relationship you have with your children.

FINANCIAL SUPPORT

The most frequently quoted contribution of fathers is financial support.

Everyone seems to naturally assume that all fathers understand the obligation to financially support their children. It's that simple, isn't it? Well, it is not simple in today's society. For instance, has anyone not heard the term "Deadbeat Dad"?

Deadbeat dad is used to describe those divorced fathers living apart from their children who fail to provide financial support for their own kids. But many non-custodial dads pay child support on a regular basis. Isn't that enough?

Let's look at the financial impact of fathers who live apart from their children, say through divorce, even when they pay child support. What would you estimate happens to the post divorce income level of the typical female head of household family? It drops about 37%! This dramatic reduction in family income affects the children most directly. Can you guess how?

Health care at all levels is less available for kids living in fatherless homes. Children without fathers pay fewer preventative visits to health care professionals. Further, when injury or illness demands treatment and medication, children living apart from their father are less likely to get all the care they need. This includes prescriptions for medications, eye glasses, physical therapy and the like.

Female single parents spend a third less time with their children in order to earn a living when compared with working, married mothers.

Without the financial support of a father, there is a restructuring of financial priorities within the family. The importance of educational goals often shared by both parents before divorce must be weighed against other financial needs and obligations. As a consequence of the reduced likelihood of a college education, the number of fatherless children dropping out of school increases. Note: about 85% of kids with both parents at home graduate from college.

Clearly, the majority of female heads of household must work. Even those single female parents who have adequate incomes spend a third less time with their children in order to earn a living, compared with working, married mothers. The vast majority of single mothers work, spend little time with their children and struggle financially. The Murphy Brown myth—that a single woman can succeed professionally and raise a child without a husband's support—might be attractive but it is more likely to put the children "at risk" educationally, emotionally and physically.

What about dads who remain with their wives and children? Fathers point to their obligations associated with wage earning as the major obstacle they face which prevents them from being more involved as fathers. Clearly, fathers must work for their families. Yet, the need to work is not an excuse for being absent as a father. A father's obligations go beyond financial support and hard work. Actively involved fathers teach their boy and girl children about their work, its value and the demands fathers must meet in the workplace. When dads take their children with them into the world of work, male children can visualize themselves as productive husbands and fathers. Female children are encouraged to be personally ambitious and learn to evaluate the qualities they will use in selecting a mate later in life.

These lessons go untaught and unlearned if father is always at work. Many children know little of dad's occupation, his skills, sacrifices and interests beyond what their mother has told them.

Not long ago, I placed an ad in a local newspaper in an attempt to learn how active dads successfully balance their work obligations with their kids' need for an involved father. To my surprise, the phone rang constantly. Some of the dads I talked with were making truly heroic efforts at being more than wage earners. Two dads stand out.

The first is Larry. Larry is a meat cutter– a butcher. Larry works for a major grocery market chain and weekends are when most families shop for food. So Larry is not available for most of his kid's weekend activities. But on his usual days off, in the middle of the week, Larry volunteers at his kids' school. He helps the teacher, eats lunch with his children and helps with homework. Larry is an older dad and there is hint of bittersweet wisdom behind his devotion to his kids. These children, a boy and girl, are his second set of children. He recalls with obvious pain the way that his first child, now a man, drifted out of his life.

The second dad who impressed me is a younger father. His name is Jim and he makes his living as a surveyor. His job often requires that he work out of town for days at a time. Jim and his wife have a daughter. She is a daddy's girl. Jim sets his alarm for 5:15 A.M. each day when he is in town so that when the child wakes up he will be ready to spend time with her. They eat, talk and then he gets her to school. When Jim is on the road, he often drives long miles, late at night so that he will be home at least every other morning! Jim tells me his wife is proud of his devotion to their child, but sometimes wonders why he goes to all the trouble. Jim points to his own dad, who Jim recalls was always "there" for him when he was a kid. These guys are Great American Heroes in my book.

Remember, dads teach through continuous interactions with the child. Children recall little of what they hear, but learn from fathers by observation—modeling.

DAD'S RULE:
The need to work is not an excuse to avoid my role as a parent.

CAREGIVING

One of the most essential contributions of fathers beyond financial support is caregiving.

At its most fundamental level, caregiving means taking care of someone who is unable to care for him or herself. Regrettably, caregiving seems universally linked to changing diapers, wiping runny noses and the like. Young fathers frequently consider it "women's work" because they associate caregiving with mothering.

The truth is caregiving for young children goes far beyond changing diapers and includes feeding, bathing, getting children to bed, helping children dress, teaching and an endless list of tasks. However, except for breast feeding, there are no gender-specific tasks related to raising a child. The notion that caregiving is not masculine is a convenient cover to mask the father's sense of incompetence.

The notion that caregiving is not masculine is most likely a convenient cover to mask the father's sense of incompetence.

Unknown to many in our country, there is a growing population of single parents who are fathers. Single parent, male-headed households represent about 14% of all single parent families. These fathers reflect all races, economic, age and education levels. They provide powerful evidence that men can balance their work obligations with the needs of their children for caring, responsive parents.

If mothers are naturally oriented towards caregiving, why is it important that dads make the effort to become caregivers as well? There are two major purposes. The first major purpose of caregiving is to anchor the father-child connection. Some child development researchers believe that following birth, very young children identify so closely with the mother that they fail to recognize that they are separate individuals. This shared identity with the mother does not exist between father and child. When the father enters the child's life through caregiving, by holding and speaking to the child, he creates a new and different identity. The father's voice, his touch, smell and laughter allow the child to shift its orientation away from the mother. The father becomes the "other me."

This process is a key developmental linkage. It initiates a relationship between father and child that points towards a different identity with the father and the outside world.

It is crucial that this linkage be established to permit the development of the next contribution—trust.

The second major purpose for a father as a caregiver is to establish himself as an equal parent with his wife. Mothers, especially new mothers, are extremely protective of their children. Further, the caregiving aspects of child rearing are often thankless and exhausting. A mother sometimes finds herself needing help, yet unwilling to trust her husband with the child. However, if the father fails to establish himself as caregiver in the early stages of the child's life, he may find that his wife will resent and distrust his efforts to assert himself or his ideas of parenting when the child is older.

A major purpose for a father as a caregiver is to establish himself as an equal parent with his wife.

Caregiving is an expression of a dad's commitment to his child. Often it is an awareness that the child needs someone, and dad is the right person for the job; that triggers masculine caregiving. Here are two examples:

Steve is the father of three very bright sons. When the second boy was an adolescent, he sustained a serious head injury as the result of an automobile accident. The son had been a star athlete and quick learner. The injury changed all that. It became apparent that the boy's recovery would be painfully slow and require countless hours of one-on-one attention. The incident was devastating for the boy's mother. She was unable to deal effectively with the easily frustrated and often difficult youth. Steve was an upper level administrator for a major corporation with a full plate of work-related responsibilities and a career moving along in the fast track.

Steve chose to work with his son. Each day, hour after hour, month after month, father and son worked, cussed, cried and laughed. Two years ago the boy, now married, received his master's degree in business. The father's career took a definite bruising but he is back on track and doing well, although he may not rise to the corporate level for which he once aimed. Would Steve do it all over again? You do not even have to guess.

Now let's talk about Allen and his nine year old daughter, Sarah. Sarah is one of those kids who drive classroom teachers nuts. She does well enough on exams, but is horribly disorganized. She loses, forgets, fails to turn in and hates homework. The inside of her backpack looks as if a hand grenade exploded in there. In short, Sarah was a mess and according to the progress reports coming home from school, about to fail everything.

After threats, rewards, screaming matches and tears, Sarah and her mom had retreated to their neutral corners. Allen, it must be admitted, was never great at academics. To be honest, he and his daughter are very alike. But maybe that was what works for them.

Each day after school, Allen and Sarah sit on the living room floor. They dump everything out of the backpack. They flatten crumpled pages, dig through and locate half completed assignments, and do what is necessary to get the job done. Sarah does not yell much at Allen. Allen is not the kind of guy you would want to yell at. Between the two of them though, Miss Sarah is about to successfully move on to the next grade in school. And it's my guess that by the time she graduates from high school, she and her dad will have learned a lot about each other and about fathering.

Effective fathers earn the trust and respect of their wives by sharing caregiving tasks throughout the child's life.

DAD'S RULE:
Caregiving is essential and is the key that opens the door to trust.

TRUST

What does it mean to trust someone?

Trust issues are extremely important to us all, both within our families and in the outside world. So what does trusting another person mean?

It means you can count on them. You can rely on them when you need help or understanding. What types of people are trustworthy?

People you can believe. People who do not tell you lies. People who will not betray you. People who are much like yourself. People you can depend on when you feel vulnerable.

An important part of learning to be a trusting person is learning who to trust.

When we think about it, trusting others can be pretty risky business. When we trust people, we more or less turn parts of our lives over to another person. Think about it. Would you trust just anyone with your life savings? Your car? Would you trust a stranger to care for your home? Your pets? To whom would you be willing to tell something personal about your life that was painful? If you were involved in a complicated problem, would you take just anyone's advice? I don't think so.

Like it or not, we run the risk of betrayal when we trust others. It is essential for us all to develop the capability for establishing and maintaining trusting relationships. And an important part of learning to be a trusting person is learning who to trust, and when it's best to trust primarily in oneself. How, then, do we teach and learn trust?

There are those who believe that the mother and child establish trust biologically. What does this mean? The mother and child share the same flesh. The mother's body is capable of feeding the child following birth. Her sympathetic nervous system remains in a heightened state of arousal for the child's first 18 to 24 months. This state of arousal allows the new mother to remain protectively vigilant during this early stage in the child's life in which babies are most vulnerable and helpless. The mother, through feeding and protection, forms powerful links of dependency and trust with her child.

Fathers do not share this biological connection with the child. Yet, fathers play a critical role in teaching the child that trusting relationships other than mother-child are valuable. The father is not the mother. His voice, style of play, touch, smell and laughter are not the same as the mother's. This, the trust established by fathers within their children, is not biological. Nor is it maternal. It is different entirely.

The formation of a trusting relationship between father and child is the first crucial experience the child will have with a representative of the outside world. It is a primary learning experience. It sets the standard against which all future trusting relationships are evaluated. It is based upon the father's *word*. The father's word is key.

Trust is established between the father and child through a kind of oral contract. Through spoken and unspoken messages, the father portrays himself as a trustworthy individual. The father is obligated to protect, care for, support and stand by the child until adulthood. It is a serious and heavy commitment.

Trust is established between the father and child through a kind of oral contract.

Importantly, it is the father's actions that either verify his trustworthiness or prove him to be a fraud. Once again, the power of the father as a teacher is linked to his behavior. The father serves as the initial and primary role model for the types of individuals, other than mothers, who can be trusted.

Some of you are probably asking, "What if a father is not trustworthy, or what if he is not ever there?" These are, of course, the critical issues. If fathers are not trustworthy (if they fail to protect, or they are abusive, or drunk) they introduce the child not to trust, but betrayal. We portray the wounds of betrayal as suspicion, fear of intimacy and self doubt.

If the father is absent entirely, or is at home infrequently, the child experiences *abandonment*. Abandonment triggers anxiety, and anxious

55

children become excessively fused or dependent upon the mother. The need for trusting relationships with persons other than the mother remains unsatisfied, plus they remain untaught and confused about how to initiate or sustain relationships outside the home. Female children attempt to form relationships through sexual interaction. Males often seek females who are willing to "mother" and direct them.

Fathers, including absent and abusive fathers, provide inescapable instructional role models for their children. Effective fathers portray the traits of individuals their children can use in determining if others in the real world are trustworthy. Male children adopt these characteristics as husbands and fathers. Female children learn to rapidly identify abusive and untrustworthy men and discontinue relationships with them.

Children learn to trust their fathers through a combination of positive and negative experiences. Earlier we talked about the father who drove late into the night to be with his daughter at least every other morning. This dad was honoring a commitment that he had made to both his child and himself.

Fathers who care enough to discipline their children also provide models for trusting relationships that are equally as powerful. The key element is consistent follow through on the father's verbal commitments.

Charlie is a very competitive dad. When his eleven year old son joined a basketball team last year, Charlie was at every practice. At every game Charlie spent the entire game yelling instructions to his son. Charlie's son, while not a natural player, was annoyed and distracted by Charlie's efforts to help.

To their credit, father and son discussed the problem after the season ended. Prior to the son's second basketball season, Charlie agreed to "not" coach during the games. He kept his word. With dad silenced on the sidelines, except for cheering, Charlie's son was more focused and productive. Both father and son had a great time. Charlie's son learned his dad could keep his word. What is more important, his son learned to trust himself.

DAD'S RULE:
When kids and Dad are not linked by trust, kids will become overly dependent on Mom.

IDENTITY

It's difficult to imagine an issue of greater importance to Americans than our personal identity!

Just think for a minute about the hundreds of ways that we identify ourselves.

We're Americans, Texans, Longhorns, Aggies. We're German, Hispanic, Irish, African-American, Asian. We are students, parents, women, husbands, sisters, engineers, electricians, Catholics, Jews, Methodists, Republicans, Democrats, sons, daughters and lovers. We are aggressive, introspective, poor, ambitious, gifted, movie lovers, slow moving, laid back, uptight and can carry a tune. I could go on and on.

'How do our children learn which, among all these words, fit them? How do words come to tell us who we are, and how is it that we ultimately choose the words we believe best describe us and which we discard? What are your hunches?

If you thought of your family, you are on the right page. Babies are like sponges, but they are far more interactive. They do "soak up" an enormous amount of information, primarily from their experiences within the family. In a fascinating way, the day to day events of a child's life are sorted, stored and integrated into his or her developing sense of identity. Naturally, the greatest source of influence on the young child is the mother.

Everyone agrees that mothers play a powerful role in the development of the child's personality. The powerful influence that mothers exert on their child's identity cannot be separated from their priorities of security, safety and comfort. Mothers emphasize sharing, avoidance of conflict, non competitive play, compliance to rules and the equal value of each family member regardless of accomplishment. Within the family there are no heroes; Mom treats weaker members with special care. She teaches personal identity within the context of family identity.

Until recently, the role of the father in formation of a child's identity has been greatly underestimated. But, the demands of life outside the safety and comfort of the family require children to develop an identity as a unique individual. Personal goals, skills and accomplishments add value and self satisfaction in a healthy identity. This is where the father enters the picture.

Even in families in which both parents work, the father portrays the obligation of each individual to identify and develop our personal interests, to test ourselves against difficult challenges, to seek personal reward through achievement and to excel. Clearly, these aspects of personal identity contrast with those associated with sharing and non competition.

Recently, I talked with a young woman who had been raised in a family along with three other sisters. Although grown, she still carries anger about her upbringing. It seems her father valued athletic competition and delighted in her performance as a child because she was a naturally gifted athlete. Her mother, however, put immense pressure on her to drop out of basketball and track because it made her older sister feel neglected by the father when she excelled.

Today in our society, boy and girl children need the influence of both parents in the formation of their identities. While many will agree that male children should profit from a close association with the father, some have difficulty understanding how a girl's identity is influenced by her father.

To explore this issue, my son Christopher recently completed a study in which he asked about 130 sixth grade boys and girls questions about their relationships with their mothers and fathers. In one question, he asked each student to indicate whether they more closely identified with the mother, the father, or with both parents equally. Chris asked me to predict if more boys than girls would identify with their fathers. I predicted that boys would more closely identify with their fathers than the girls. Surprisingly, I was wrong! About 55% of twelve-year old boys, living with both mother and father, reported a closer relationship with dad. However, 67% of the girls in the study indicated that they were more like their fathers than their mothers!

These results lend verification to the notion that females strongly identify with their fathers.

Fathers need to initiate activities with children away from home and without mother. Fathers are likely to take their youngsters beyond the comfort zone, testing and challenging the child. At times, the child may experience frustration, disappointment and failure. Things may go badly. That's the way life is. Dad's role is to help them absorb life's disappointments and develop a willingness to come back for more.

Inevitably, Father and Mother will probably disagree about how much is too much of a challenge. Such disagreements are not only unavoidable; they are healthy. When children are aware that Mom and Dad have strong, if different, views, they also learn that neither perspective is always right or wrong. A father must neither avoid his role, or attempt to bully Mom into backing away from hers.

A father must neither avoid his role, or attempt to bully Mom into backing away from hers.

Dads who are uninvolved rob their children of the opportunity to share the diversity of both parents' perspectives, attitudes, values, opinions and experiences. There is an old saying, "A child needs to know and be known by the father." When children are familiar with and understand their father, they absorb his values. When the father takes the time to really know his child, that child's sense of personal identity is verified and strengthened.

Without the father's contribution, the child is likely to identify too closely with the mother and may find the challenges associated with career identification, competitive situations and personal achievement overwhelming.

DAD'S RULE:
A child needs to know and be known by the father.

FAMILY TRADITIONS

Do you understand the value of family traditions? What are the traditional things that your family does year after year? Often, traditions are associated with religious celebrations. Some seem to be seasonal, like going to the beach or football games.

Traditions have played a much more powerful role in the lives of past generations and older cultures than they play now. It has been my experience that even caring fathers get pulled away from the children because of work and other obligations.

For these fathers, traditions are a treasure. Wise fathers have learned to use traditions as a way of staying connected with their children.

Traditions link us to our past, to the people we loved, to experiences, memories. They remind us of our shared heritage, our roots. They are repeated in the here and now. And we can see ourselves doing the same things in the future. Traditions provide a continuity.

Traditions anchor and reconnect fathers with their children. Traditions, such as cutting Christmas trees or Dad's famous silver dollar pancakes on Sunday morning allow the father to step back into the life of his children. Traditions provide a way for dads to overcome obstacles and maintain important linkages.

Traditions anchor or reconnect fathers with their children.

A divorced father I know, each Wednesday, sits on the floor with his son and together they dump his school backpack on the floor and reorganize it. They have done this now for five years because it works. It works to keep the boy organized and it works to show the child that his father cares. Traditions like this allow the child to see him or herself in a future that includes the father. It is a secure vision.

Traditions are part of many religious rituals, but they can be created with surprising ease. Children are, by nature, comfortable with repetitious patterns of life. Children also are easily "welded" to spontaneous and emotionally charged events.

At times traditions are created in a spontaneous way when the magnetism of Dad's humor or enjoyment of an event combines with his kids' yearning to take part in the action. In one family, year after year, the father and son spend several full weekends gathering and splitting firewood for the family's fireplace. In another family, Thanksgiving means the traditional touch football game with Dad, uncle and kids huffing and puffing. Another dad turned summer hikes into reed gathering and basket making lessons, which a college girl recently confessed she looked forward to (even though she would never admit it).

Of all the contributions dads can make with their children, traditions are by far the easiest and least seldom used. It is a puzzlement. It's so easy. If kids like doing something, anything with Dad...just pay attention and do it again. There are more examples than I can possibly provide. Here are two very brief ones.

Bill is the father of two college aged kids, one male and one female. When they were kids, he would take them hiking. Hiking was something he liked to do. This is very important. Dads have to like the activity. Anyway, on these hikes Bill would point out all sorts of plants and other things. In particular, he would have them find and gather certain types of branches. Later, after the hike, Bill would show the kids how to artfully weave the twigs into baskets.

So, last Christmas the daughter, now a freshman in college, returned home with gifts for the whole family. When dad opened his rather oddly shaped package, he found a bundle of sticks! It turns out that while the daughter was on work detail to gather firewood for a traditional football bonfire, she had found herself searching for dad's favorite basket making branches. After Christmas dinner, there they sat, Bill and his almost grown college daughter weaving twigs into baskets.

My second example involves a man whose name I do not know. He came up to me following one of my workshops with fathers in which I had talked about father-child traditions. Years ago, when his son was about six or seven, he started taking him camping. Actually, the dad and his brother had camped all their lives and mutually decided to take their kids along. The plan was not to have a plan. They just drove in some direction until they found a place to camp. Apparently, there were times when the strategy worked better than others. The trips were adventures in the truest sense. But what the guy's son loved best, and the thing that he couldn't wait to tell mom about after the trip was not having to take a bath for a whole week!

DAD'S RULE:

Traditions are a golden opportunity waiting for fathers to reconnect with their children.

SECURITY

Families are intended to provide safety and security for their members. What is it that we typically think about when we focus on security issues? Of course. Maintaining our safety from outsiders. The outside world can be dangerous, and parents must provide protection for their children.

There is also another, equally important, form of security. I am talking about the father's role of insuring the security of family members within the family.

For families to function they must not only keep their members safe from outside harm, but create a secure environment in which children and others feel safe living within the family. As you are aware, this internal safety does not exist within many American families.

There is alarming evidence that a large percentage of women and children experience physical and sexual abuse by their own family members. Men are often responsible for injuring less powerful members of their family. As a consequence, fathers are often identified as a source of threat rather than security. Within families of every race, economic and educational level, fathers are viewed as drunken, brutal individuals, capable of using power rather than reason to control family members, yet unwilling or incapable of exercising self control of their own emotions or sexual urges.

The father provides a role model for his children by governing his behaviors with them and his wife.

In contrast, effective fathers play dual roles within the family to establish and maintain security. First, the father provides a role model for his children by governing his behaviors with them and his wife. Male children learn respect for women by observing the behaviors of the father during heated interactions between the mother and dad. Effective fathers refuse to fall victim to their angry emotions, resist physical impulses and set a standard for family interactions.

These fathers also model and rehearse self control with children through physical play such as roughhousing. Everyone knows about roughhousing, right? Boy and girl children love to pile on Dad. Typically, it drives moms nuts; but think about what is happening when grown men play roughly with children.

Consider the size and body weight of an average adult male. How tall are grown men? How much do most men weigh? Now, compare them to the average five-or seven-year-old; or even bigger kids. What do you notice about the differences in size and weight? What does common sense tell you about strength differences? What do these very obvious differences between grown men and children teach us about self control and limits when the play is rough, fun and, yet, no one is getting hurt? That's right! The father obviously is controlling both himself and the child at once!

"Look: we can play rough, we can act wild and crazy, we can be physical and I am not hurting you."

The message is clear. The father communicates, verbally or without saying anything, "Look: we can play rough, we can act wild and crazy, we can be physical and I am not hurting you." The powerful message is that fathers control themselves!

Importantly, through rough play the father also teaches a second major lesson. Through safe but rigorous play the father is saying, "Not only will I not hurt you, but I am not going to allow you to injure me." The message is not that fathers are so tough that they cannot be hurt. The message to the child is: "You must learn to contain your impulses or we will stop playing."

Effective fathers establish clear limits for the child's behavior. Within these limits the child and other family members can feel secure. Beyond them, the father will contain out of control behaviors. Limits provide children with a sense of security and caring. Limits insure self respect and teach respect for others. The real world is intolerant of children (of whatever age) who are unable to control their impulses.

> Recently, a young couple talked with me about their youngest of two sons. This boy is a real pistol! He is three going on twenty-three; smart, strong willed and fearless. The mother was on the verge of collapse. "When I'm alone with him, he will not behave. What annoys me is that when his father comes home he doesn't pull the stuff he does with me!"
>
> When asked, the boy's father agreed, "He is a handful. There is no doubt about that. The main difference between the way I deal with him and she does, is that she takes every thing he does personally and I don't.

Sometimes my wife gets rattled when he gets mad because he's not getting his way. But the way I look at it is with anybody that strong willed there's no way he's not going to get mad, besides you can't let a three-year-old run the show."

The issue is security, in this case, helping the young mother become more secure with her ability to maintain limits. Clearly, in this situation the father will be of benefit to her as she gains confidence. In other situations, the mother may assume the leadership role.

DAD'S RULE:

When father sets and maintains reasonable limits, their children feel secure within the family and behave themselves outside it.

SELF PROTECTION

We cannot live our lives nestled perpetually within the security of our families. Neither can we expect that our parents will accompany us into the real world to provide protection. Like it or not, everyone in our society must learn to be self protective.

Within families, teaching self protection is often not a priority. Mothers are quick to protect their young. Mothers emphasize the avoidance of individuals and situations that threaten their children. They value sharing and family ownership of possessions. Life inside the family is not necessarily like life in the real world.

The real world does not respect unprotected boundaries. You are familiar with the word "boundaries", right? Think about its typical use. That's right, property is defined by its boundaries. We sometimes also think of boundaries as barriers that keep outsiders from getting inside.

The real world does not respect unprotected boundaries.

Now think of how boundaries apply to ourselves and our lives. Think of your personal boundaries. If you are having trouble with this notion, think about the types of personal or private things that we may not wish to share with others, or which we may need to protect. Does that make it easier? Yes, of course, our bodies: "I will not be touched without permission." Our identity. Our possessions. Our emotions. Our ideas. Our accomplishments. All of these things have boundaries that we must protect.

In all our lives, events may happen which threaten our boundaries. No matter how much parents love, protect and hope for their children's success, they will definitely encounter other individuals who will attempt to violate their boundaries. Three of five females experience sexual abuse.

Trusted employees discover that coworkers have reported them to supervisors for misdeeds of which they are innocent. Senior citizens are beaten and robbed. We need to be able to take care of ourselves.

Make no mistake: self protection must be taught. Effective fathers play key roles in teaching their children to protect themselves, their money, possessions and good name. Once again, role modeling is the primary means of instruction.

A mother provided this example. Her son had received a new bicycle and insisted on riding it to school. On the way home, he stopped by his buddy's house to show it off and while he was inside the friend's home, some other kid rode off on his bike. Well, the boy was heartbroken and panicked about what his parents would say to him. So the mom was being a good mother by consoling the boy and telling him not to worry, that they would call the police and report the theft. But when the dad got home, he put the boy in his car and they drove up and down streets until they found the kid on the boy's bike. Now this is important...the dad had his son confront the kid and make him give back the bike. The mother was impressed with her husband and the boy learned a valuable lesson from his dad.

The lessons of self protection can include some tasks that may not make Dad a popular guy.

The lessons of self protection can include some tasks that may not make Dad a popular guy. One such lesson is teaching our kids to care for their possessions. Raising children is very expensive. Clothing is expensive as well as all the other things kids need and want. Sporting equipment, tennis shoes, and computer games cost a lot of money.

While children are usually insistent that parents buy things for them, once the things are at home they lose their value. Kids lose everything...toys, clothes, everything. What they do not lose, they "lend" to their friends.

Effective, but sometimes unpopular, dads employ The Father's Rule: I will buy the first jacket, basketball, etc., but if you lose it, you buy the next one. This sounds harsh, but it is very effective. At times, however, father's attempts to emphasize the child's need to be self protective run counter to mom's desire to keep her children comfortable and well cared for. Actually both parents need to play out their roles, so the conflict is a healthy indication that both are doing their jobs.

When we think about self protection, many men have asked how dads go about teaching their boys and girls to be self protective. As always, many of my examples are basically common sense responses. Consider these.

While many fathers admonish their children to "take up" for themselves, they fail to provide teaching experiences that allow the kids to see how self protection works. I talked with a young woman who had been involved in an abusive relationship. I asked if her father was a brutal man. The woman assured me that her father had been kind and caring to her as a child. I pressed the issue by asking if her mother had valued such a sensitive man as her husband. The young woman's eyes filled with tears as she confided that her father was beaten down by his wife's sharp and critical tongue lashings.

This father, while loving, betrayed his daughter. He failed to portray himself in a self protective manner. Understand: Fathers are not required to win each and every argument with their spouses. They are not required to dominate women. They are required to take care of themselves. Our children are watching. If Dad maintains his boundaries, his children will be more capable to do so as well.

Here is a second example. Self protection also means taking care of our belongings. We must be ready to protect our belongings from others. And there are times when our kids need to learn to protect their belongings from their own carelessness.

Consider the incident in which the boy's new bicycle had been stolen. The boy came inside and when he went back outside, the bike had been taken. The mom said that she and the boy were both very upset. The boy was yelling, "It's gone! I'll never get it back!" The mom was trying to console the kid and was about to call the police when dad arrived at the family home.

Upon hearing the details, Dad told the boy to get in the car. The two of them drove up and down the neighborhood streets until they spotted the bike with some strange kid riding it. The dad pulls the car right up to the bicycle and instructs his son to tell the kid to get off the bike or he'll haul his butt to jail. End of story.

Now, here's another example. A father sets down a contract with his son. The contract is simple and straight forward. When the father agrees to buy something for the boy like a winter jacket or a basketball, the boy agrees to take care of it. That is, not leave it on the school bus or playground. If the son "forgets" and the article is "lost," the boy buys the replacement or does without it.

So the father buys his son an expensive jacket. The son leaves it at the bus stop. And now some other kid has an expensive new jacket. A few days later, it is cold. The boy suddenly remembers the jacket. If the father or mother caves in, what does the boy learn? As it turns out, the boy buys his own jacket. It's not as expensive, but it is warm, and he does not lose it.

DAD'S RULE:

I buy the first one...If you lose it, you pay for the new one.

HUMOR

Within families, children are valued without having to earn their parents' love through accomplishments or merit. At least, that's the mythology we attempt to sustain. In real life, success is more closely linked to our competence and performance. Preparing children for life outside the family requires that parents emphasize performance through experiences that help the child make the connection between personal skills and success.

Competitive situations that challenge individuals to aim toward peak performance levels help us fine tune our skills. But there is a negative side to competition. What is this predictable emotional spin-off of situations in which an individual's performance is tested? Exactly: Stress, pressure—or what psychologists call "performance anxiety."

Performance anxiety results when we sense that everyone is watching to see how well or poorly we do while competing. It's a fearful feeling that we will not measure up; that we will let down our parents, friends and ourselves.

When anxiety is very high, our performance drops below our capability.

When performance anxiety is very high what do you think happens to performance? Does it get better or worse when anxiety is intense? Exactly. When performance anxiety is very high, our performance drops below our capability. Athletes become wooden, puppet-like. Students go blank, forgetting things they have studied for hours.

So what does all this have to do with fathers? Well, it has to do with humor.

Let's not forget that Dad's role is linked to his child's preparation for life in the real world. This means that dads often place an emphasis on the child's performance, which can trigger anxiety.

Effective dads use their own failures or less than perfect past performances as tension breakers, allowing kids to be self forgiving and less anxious. Humorous stories are more powerful teaching tools with children than are lectures. Lectures turn kids off. Funny stories capture their imagination.

Here is an example. When my father was in high school, he and his parents lived on a ranch in a remote, hill country region of Texas. On one occasion, my dad wanted to use the family's old truck to drive many miles to his high school dance. My grandmother objected because of the distance my dad would have to drive using winding narrow roads and because she feared he would be tempted by older boys drinking beer.

My grandfather insisted that he go, but in a stern voice gave my dad these instructions: "Listen, go to the dance and stay as late as you want. And if you get a chance to drink beer, I want you to go ahead and drink as much as you can hold. Then when you're coming home, I want you to drive that old truck just as fast as you can. When you come to the top of a steep hill, just step on the gas. That way if you leave the road and hit a tree, you'll be killed outright. It would break your mother's heart if you had to live your whole life as a cripple!"

My father loved that story. He told this same story to me when I was a teenager. Incidentally, neither of us ever wrecked a car because we were drinking!

There is one other point I want to discuss about humor and that's its connection with playfulness. I have said that Dad's unique role is aimed at preparing his child for real life. Well, from a child's perspective, play is a reflection of real life. Play is about making rules and breaking them. It's about playing hard, inventing reality, trying on roles. Play is about winning, losing and sometimes getting hurt. Once a kid I had in my office who said to his mother, "If you're going to play, you're going to get hurt. But, Mom, you gotta play!"

When fathers enter the child's reality through play, they gain access to a powerful teaching tool. Play is a magnet that draws children closer to their fathers. Their silliness allows both to take off to unimaginable, if absurd, heights of creativity.

Dad's unique role is aimed at preparing his child for real life. From a child's perspective, play is a reflection of real life.

DAD'S RULE:
Lectures turn kids off; humor pulls them in and reduces anxiety.

COURAGE

The next contribution of fathers is courage.

When we think of courageous acts, what thoughts come to mind?

Typically, we think of bravery, of heroism. We think of heroic individuals fearlessly taking charge in dangerous situations. I guess everybody naturally loves hearing about heroic acts.

I can still vividly picture a young man leaping through the falling snow

THE COMMON SENSE NO-FRILLS, PLAIN-ENGLISH GUIDE TO BEING A SUCCESSFUL DAD

into the frozen river to rescue a drowning female passenger who was the victim of an airplane disaster in Washington, D.C. several years ago.

I am certain that just about everyone can remember at least one courageous person or heroic act that fills us with the feelings of admiration and pride.

Most of us will never personally experience such events in our lifetimes. However, as a psychologist, my experience has taught me that men and women can expect to face threatening life situations in which they must behave courageously. There is nothing that I know of—not wealth, faith in God, advanced degrees, a seemingly secure job position—not one of these things exempts us from times in which threat is unavoidable.

You are familiar with such real life situations, aren't you? There is the threat of losing your job or having to deal with unreasonable supervisors. There is the threat of betrayal, of being physically injured by lawless people, of life threatening illness, of losing loved ones.

We are not talking about situations that call for impulsive acts of heroism. They are however, situations that demand we stand up for ourselves and deal with difficult and complex events.

We can measure true courage by our willingness to persevere even when faced with frustration, complexity, defeat and difficulty.

Life is difficult. The lesson taught by heroic, yet ordinary people, is that the measure of courage is our willingness to persevere even when faced with frustration, complexity and defeat. Courageous individuals may not appear in newspapers as national heroes, but their resilience to setbacks allows them set goals, overcome obstacles and accept life's challenges.

Effective fathers encourage their children to take calculated risks and test themselves. They allow their children to experience success and on occasion, defeat. Men tend to be competitive. And everyone knows that if we are going to compete, we have to earn our place on the team and that sometimes our opponents will outscore us.

When children experience exhaustion, hard work and the need for repetitive practice, they often want to quit. Effective fathers are willing to work with their kids. But the option of quitting just because things are tough is not allowed.

When fathers react to threat triggered by the mother's anger by always giving in, they lose credibility in the eyes of their children.

When fathers insist that the child stay with the situation, even though things are going as well as expected, mothers sometime attempt to rescue the child. It is not unusual for a well meaning mother to challenge her husband and become angry if he appears not to share her need to keep the child safe and comfortable.

However, learning to deal with life's adversities is essential. When fathers understand the source of their wife's anger, and yet stand by the legitimacy of their obligation to help the child learn to persevere, they

68

model courageous behavior for their children. When fathers react to their wife's anger by always giving in, they lose credibility in the eyes of their children. Clearly, neither mothers nor fathers are always correct and they are both obligated to learn from and understand each other's perspective. However, many fathers are afraid of women's anger and disenfranchise themselves by running from conflict even when their beliefs are valid.

There are two types of courage that deserve emphasis. The first is the courage to persevere when success is neither immediate nor gained easily. We have already talked about an example of this type of courage. Think again about Steve and his son who had sustained a brain injury. Consider what the experience must have been like for the boy. The brain injury did not reduce his long term memory. He remembered perfectly well that once, not long ago, school had been a cake walk. The walls of his room were covered with photos of him with fellow athletes; his shelves with trophies.

How do we measure the courage of this boy to return to his same school one year later and repeat the grade level? On what scale do we judge his willpower as he walked the halls with a cane? We only know that his father dropped him off and picked him up each day. We know that Steve would not allow him to be placed in special classes. We know that they became a team.

Because this example involves an injured boy, do not make the mistake of concluding that most kids do not need to learn about perseverance. They do.

A second type of courage is demanded if we are to live a full and satisfying life. This is the courage to accept calculated risks. Regardless of our sex we all come across situations in which we must choose between action and passivity. Here is an example.

A young girl is nominated for a school honor. Because her twin sister is not nominated, their mother believes she should refuse the award. The girl wants to accept, but does not want to anger the mother. She appeals to her father, who will not make the decision for her, but promises to support her decision. The girl chooses to accept the honor. The father makes her do her own talking, but stands beside her decision. The mother is angry with both of them, but the girl earns the recognition she deserves. Her real trophy is the courage she feels within her.

DAD'S RULE:

Courage means moving beyond comfort...helping kids to test themselves and to persevere.

INDEPENDENCE

Think about families. Specifically, think back to our earlier discussion about the roles mothers typically play within families. Consider what I discovered when I met with a group of about twenty mothers at an elementary school. We were talking about the need for fathers to play active caregiver roles for the children. While most of the moms had no argument with the "idea" of dads being caregivers, they readily acknowledged that their view of raising children meant doing "everything" for their children. When asked what "everything" included, their lists went far beyond the basic feeding, dressing and the like. When they said everything, they really meant everything.

I am not critical of these mothers. They were doing their job. That's the good news. The bad news? When mothers do everything, when they are caregiver, social chairman, spokesman, arbitrator, protector and rescuer, the children may stay safe and comfortable, but they also become very dependent. The bad news is that dependent children remain incompetent at knowing how to take care of themselves.

The bad news is that dependent children remain incompetent.

Think about what happens to dependent adults in our country. Boomerang children return to their parent's home, often with children they cannot support. Many cannot hold down jobs. Others live on welfare. These individuals personify incompetence and live out their lives as children-like adults.

Life demands that we provide for our own needs.

When children have an active father, they are less dependent on the mother. In contrast to doing everything for the child, father's rule is: Don't do for children what they can do for themselves.

Don't do for the children what they can do for themselves.

Once, when my son was about six, he had spent the day at the home of his best friend. I went to pick him up and found him and his buddy running around barefooted. We were gathering his belongings, and I said, "Christopher, put on your shoes." Chris sat down on the floor, but before he could get started, his friend's mom pulled on his socks and was tying his shoes for him.

I said, "Aimee, Christopher knows how to tie his shoes. Why are you doing that?" She said, "I never though about it, I tie all my kid's shoes out of habit." Aimee is a great mother, but always doing things for kids is not necessarily in the kids best interest.

It's important for dads to schedule time alone with their kids when mom is not around. When dads initiate these activities, kids typically get a lot more practice doing things for themselves. When fathers introduce their children to new experiences (like building a fort, or snow skiing) things are going to go wrong. By staying alert, dads can guide youngsters through challenging tasks. They work with the child and explain, rather than criticize. At other times dads do not do things according to mom's rules.

Remember, mothers are powerful rule setters. Their rules create a protective web around children to insure their safety. When dads initiate activities with their kids, mom's rules may be challenged. Many believe that the process of becoming an individual begins when dads urge their children to accept challenges and take calculated risks.

> *A perfect example of this point comes from a father named Chad who responded to one of my newspaper ads. Chad, it seems has had a long standing love affair with canoes, rivers and white water rapids. At one time Chad dreamed of camping and river running with his sons. An apparent obstacle arose when Chad and his wife had three girls!*
>
> *Chad solved the problem by becoming a campfire girl parent and taking the whole group of girls on river trips. One of his daughters became a competitive "kayak-er" and another has her master's degree in fresh water biology. Chad reported that his daughters learned to master white water rapids, although he had a more difficult time convincing their mother that he did not intend to drown them.*

I have learned that, whenever possible, successful fathers allow the child to correct his or her own mistakes and avoid jumping into rescue the child prematurely. It takes patience, but the payoffs are an increased sense of self awareness and self confidence by the child.

DAD'S RULE:
Don't do for children what children can do for themselves.

SELF CONFIDENCE

> *Recently, I worked with a high school golfer who was having major self confidence problems. During tournament play, if he made a poor shot, he would go ballistic. He would slam his club into the ground and kick his bag. As often as not, he was unable to recover. His negativity worsened as the season progressed and the golf coach was very close to dropping him*

from the team. Although his practice rounds placed him as one of his team's most skilled players, his uneven tournament play barely justified maintaining him on the varsity team.

When we first talked, the high-schooler was very self critical. He referred to himself as a loser. He employed a host of self condemning terms to explain his experience of failure. He did not know what to do differently.

Amazingly, the young athlete and I did not meet for many sessions. We did not have to. We hit on what was going on pretty quickly, made a couple of changes and they worked. He went on to place second, as a sophomore, in the State Golf Tournament. Can you guess what we discovered?

Here's how we approached his self confidence issues. We knew that in practice rounds, during which the coach made the varsity team members compete with each other to qualify for tournament play, he did very well. When he made poor shots, he would become briefly angry, but he was able to recover nicely. When we compared practice rounds with tournament play, the one difference that absolutely jumped out at us was the presence of you know who...Good old Dad!

Now this dad was devoted to his son. And the son clearly yearned for his father's admiration. But the father was unable to disconnect himself from his son's performance. During tournament play, the father was a man of a thousand facial gestures. Good shots would trigger war whoops; poor shots would send him stomping away. Although there are rules that disallow adults from actually talking to players, his body language gave a critique of every shot, club selection and even how the son walked down the fairway.

The teenager taught me a powerful lesson about father-child relationships. He wanted his father to watch him, but not his criticism.

I suggested that maybe Dad should just stay home during tournament play. But the teenager taught me a powerful lesson about father-child relationships. He wanted his father to watch him. He wanted his dad to see him play. What he needed though, was for his father to let him play his own game, win or lose. He wanted his father's presence, but not his criticism.

With some difficulty we talked to Dad about what we had learned. In truth, this was not what Dad wanted to hear, but he did acknowledge that he probably got a little over involved. We recruited Mom to help the father become more aware of his behavior, and he learned to contain his emotions. The rest, as they say, is history.

Life demands that we learn how we learn. To master new skills, we have to be able to enter novel and difficult situations believing that we can succeed.

We call this trust in our abilities self confidence.

How do we gain self confidence in our abilities?

You guessed right. Self confidence is learned. Learning occurs when we are able to connect what we are doing with what happens to us as a result of our behaviors. This demands self awareness. Criticism, in contrast, disconnects our focused attention and replaces it with confusion.

Criticism, in contrast, disconnects our focused attention and replaces it with confusion.

DAD'S RULE:

Coach with out criticism. Criticism kills self confidence.

When fathers introduce their children to real life experiences, they take on the role of teacher or coach. Master teachers have taught us that the most productive form of teaching is corrective instruction. This means that the student is allowed to make mistakes. The role of the father/coach is to fine tune his child's responses. This process of fine tuning demands that the coach stay focused on the behaviors and not become critical of the child. When fathers are super critical of their children, they become the biggest obstacles to their kids' learning and performance. Effective fathers understand that support and approval do more to build self confidence than so-called constructive criticism.

PATIENCE

What do you think is one of the most difficult yet a beneficial contribution a father can offer a child?

If you named patience, you are correct.

Life demands that we learn as quickly as we are capable. The attainment of new skills does not necessarily come easily. Typically mastering new skills requires repeated practice to reduce mistakes. But as we have seen, many dads have a hard time with their kids' mistakes. When fathers respond to mistakes with anger, performance anxiety goes up, short term memory goes down and learning is slowed. Further, kids tend to avoid angry adults and so Dad's power as a teacher diminishes. And finally, a parent's intolerance for mistakes leads to perfectionistic and self critical thinking by his children.

Children learn to persevere when dads are patient.

In contrast, kids learn perseverance when mistakes and disappointments are balanced against the father's patience. When dads respond to unintended errors calmly and without catastrophe, children adopt the father's model. Children learn to persevere when dads are patient.

A key factor in becoming more patient is linked to our expectations.

Children learn to persevere when dads are patient.

When fathers understand that kids are not perfect and that mistakes are to be expected, they are less likely to fall into the trap of impatience.

I have discovered that impatient and critical fathers are often unsure of their own abilities to correct their child's mistakes. The more confident Dad is in teaching new skills, the greater patience he will display.

But just as dads cannot expect their kids to be perfect, neither should he demand perfection of himself. Fathers are the representatives of the outside world. Real life is not always fair, and dads are not always patient, courageous, understanding or available when kids need them.

DAD'S RULE:
___

As dad's demonstrate more patience their kids become better, faster learners.

Wise dads acknowledge that they do not always know every answer. Dads capable of forgiving themselves for being imperfect are able to offer their children forgiveness.

As children grow older, dads often become much like coaches. The father-child relationship is complex, however. The child yearns for the father's approval and when dads are impatient, their words can wound the child. It is important for dads to remember that patience is part of their power as a teacher. When Dad is over-reactive, when he barks at mistakes or interrupts his child's imperfect attempts at new task, he robs his child of the opportunity to become a "self starter." Here's an example.

A friend of mine is one of those guys who can fix anything. Every time I call him, he is working on some project around his home or someone else's. More often than not, he got one of his three kids involved. Now most dads I know are always complaining about how they can never get their kids involved in anything that even remotely sounds like work.

When I asked him to tell me his secret, he said, "It's simple. Kids want to do stuff, not just watch. But when most dads try to let them do something like sawing boards for example, they either skip the 'demo' phase or they don't understand that it's important to back off and let the kid work at it. A lot of guys don't show the kid how it's done, they just get mad as hell when the kids mess up. I've just learned when to demonstrate and when to back off. It's really just common sense."

FORGIVENESS

I want to tell you about an incident that happened between my son

Christopher and me. We are very much alike. We share many character traits, both good and bad. And perhaps as a consequence, we get angry with each other and argue. Now, I hold strongly to the belief that the roots of relationships are deepened when family members can argue about issues without tearing away at each other. But, there are times when I am forced very nearly to eat my words.

For about a week, Chris and I had been arguing and arguing. I cannot remember exactly what about. It was probably something that he felt a twelve-year-old should be allowed to do, and I did not endorse his idea. Anyway, by the end of the week, we were at gridlock and we were both angry.

We were driving home together Friday evening. I was tired from working and exhausted from my running argument with Chris. I must have absentmindedly groaned out loud, because Chris said, "What is that about?" "I'm just unhappy about our relationship right now," I said. "It seems like all you and I do anymore is fuss at each other." There was a pause, then Chris said, "I thought that when people love each other, they can be mad and not have to worry that the other person will stop loving them." Chris was correct. We also have to learn to resolve our differences, but he hit the forgiveness nail right on the head.

Life comes with its share of disappointments, and often disappointment triggers frustration and anger. Because dads are imperfect, we can let our children down.

Forgiveness allows us to let go of disappointment and anger.

Forgiveness allows us to let go of disappointment and anger.

DAD'S RULE:

When dads acknowledge and accept that things are not perfect they can teach kids to adapt to life's realities through self acceptance.

There are some things about life that are magical. One of them is forgiveness. Forgiveness allows us to be accepting of our wives, our children and ourselves. The process begins when fathers are willing to acknowledge their own imperfections.

Unforgiving fathers, fathers unwilling to admit to their own flaws, seem to smolder with resentment for their children. They do not teach their children much about forgiveness. Instead, they teach that fathers are cold, perfectionist and frightening.

In contrast, the traits most admired by adult women who had available, caring fathers were those of emotional steadiness and forgiveness. When, as youngsters, they had made mistakes and things seemed to be getting too emotional, it was the father's emotional containment and willingness to forgive that remained in their memories.

Fathers do not have to be special. Children almost never view truly effective dads as heroic. Most of the time these dads are too familiar to be regarded as special. They are just dads.

Forgiving fathers open the door for their children to learn self forgiveness. Self forgiveness allows children to admit their mistakes and to become self correcting.

Forgiving fathers open the door for their children to learn self forgiveness. Self forgiveness allows children to acknowledge their mistakes and to become self correcting.

Want to learn how to teach your child to tell lies? Be unforgiving. The lessons taught by parents whose children deny wrong doing even when caught in the act, all point to families lacking forgiveness.

I have discovered that fathers who are willing to acknowledge their own mistakes are a lot more willing to empathize with their children. One father told me that his father-in-law disapproved when the dad admitted his imperfections to his children. Apparently, the father-in-law believed that fathers somehow weaken their influence by acknowledging personal errors.

This is an insecure position, which ignores the axiom that wisdom comes from having learned from our share of blunders and misjudgments.

BEFORE MOVING ON

I want to review a few key things we have discussed:

- Kids need the balance of a mother and a father.
- If a father is absent the consequences are profound.
- Moms tend to teach by rule setting, nurturing, protecting and affiliation.
- Dads continue to represent the outside world. To put it another way, dads help kids learn how to deal with life outside the security of the home.

As you have discovered, the contributions of mothers and fathers may overlap. Yet, it is my belief that men and women do not parent their children in the same way. Further, while it might be possible for mothers to behave like fathers, in most instances they do not. Even the best of mothers cannot be substitute fathers.

Children need active fathers. The mother's role is essential and powerful. The father's role is not the same as that of the mother, but it is no less essential. The fathers' and mothers' roles are complementary.

Remember, my attempt has not been to create the profile of an ideal father. Instead, it's been my intent to provide bench marks for fathers, against which to measure themselves. Think about the contributions that we have covered. Are you already doing these things? I hope so.

What I have found is that making these contributions is not always easy. In some cases, dads may not have the skills. In other cases, dads may not know how to get started. And finally, dads often run into obstacles that make being a father difficult.

Nonetheless, the opportunity to be a real father to your children is an open door waiting for you to walk through. The pay off for your kids will be measured in their ability to deal with life as capable adults. Life is tough and so there are no guarantees of success. But kids with active dads–available dads–are likely to be resilient, perseverent, self protective and self confident. These are human traits that cannot be purchased.

4

What's *a*

MOTHER

to *Do?*

What's A Mother To Do?

Mom, this chapter is for you. Dad, keep reading as well. It's been my intent to emphasize the need children have for a balance between a mother and a father. Yet, many of today's fathers did not have adequate fathers to them to teach them how to be fathers. As a consequence, I have discovered a generation of confused men struggling to carve out their roles as fathers.

One thing that can facilitate the process of becoming an effective dad is the support of the mother. However, when mothers fail to understand what dad is attempting, for example when the mother did not have an effective father herself, she can become a major obstacle to her husband's attempts. Mothers sometimes act as gatekeepers, monitoring the father's access to their children. In her book, *Women and Their Fathers*, Victoria Secunda writes that mothers, at the moment of birth, assume sole ownership of the child. This ownership gives her the power to restrict access of others to their child, including the father.

I have observed that while some mothers complain that their husbands fail to play active roles in the lives of their children, they simultaneously criticize and belittle their husbands' efforts. These mothers justify their criticism because the fathers are clumsy or do things differently.

Researchers have found that neither first time mothers nor first time fathers are very competent in dealing with their newborn baby. By the end of the first year, however, most new moms are far more competent than fathers. The obvious reason is that the moms have had a lot more practice. The most effective dads, however, are those who play shared roles with their wives in caregiving for children. This caregiving serves a variety of purposes.

One purpose, for example, is that masculine caregiving establishes the

Mothers sometimes act as gatekeepers, monitoring the father's access to their children.

mother's trust for the dad. This trusting relationship allows her to relax and let dad play out his role. However, not knowing this, most young fathers allow the mother to do everything. Later, if these fathers decide to become more active, they discover that they have not earned the mom's trust. Lacking practice, many are incompetent and most are frustrated. They do not have the practiced ease and fluidity when dealing with the youngster that the mother does.

This chapter begins by acknowledging the powerful role moms play. Dads need their support in their efforts to be better fathers. Moms play essential roles in the lives of their children. The relationship between the husband and the wife is equally powerful in determining how effective the father can be as an equal parent.

So Moms, if you fail to understand or agree with what Dad is attempting, there are going to be problems. However, if you endorse and support Dad's efforts, your children will benefit. A word of caution: I do not expect you to agree with everything Dad is attempting to do. At times, you probably will strongly disagree. In this chapter, as we did in Part 3, we will discuss each of the 13 contributions of effective dads. We will look at these "contributions" from the perspective of both the mother and father. I am certain that some things may trigger your displeasure. Controversy is thought provoking.

Recently, psychologists have been attempting to discover what mothers and fathers do that is truly unique. There seem to be certain essential characteristics of parenting, such as good judgment, understanding, and empathy that both mothers and fathers share. However, if we peel away the layers, we discover that the ways in which mothers show empathy for their children are not the same ways that fathers show empathy. Likewise, the ways that fathers earn their children's trust are not the same ways that mothers establish trust. In short, fathers are not the same as mothers.

I will briefly introduce each contribution, and then Gay Klinger, my partner, the mother of our son and my wife for nearly 20 years will comment. Gay is also a family counselor. We have worked together for almost 15 years. Gay has done dozens of workshops with mothers around issues associated with father-child relationships. She brings not only her personal and clinical insights to this dialogue, but also insights she has gained from other moms as well. Let's talk about how mothers view the contributions that dads make, and how they can support those contributions.

WHAT'S A MOTHER TO DO?

FINANCIAL SUPPORT

Ron: The issue of financial support presents a paradox. What I mean is
that financial support is the most frequently mentioned contribution that fathers make to their families. At the same time, when I
asked dads about the obstacles that prevent them from being active
fathers, the necessity to spend time earning a living is at the top of
the list. So we have two seemingly contradictory things happening
simultaneously — the need to earn money and the need to be a
dad. In most cases, dads believe that their primary obligation is to
provide money for their families.

I have found that many fathers of today get carried away with
wage earning. I have run into dads who have two and three jobs.
Some dads have jobs that take them away from home 51 weeks out
of the year! In other cases, dads have jobs that keep them in foreign
countries for nine and ten months of the year. What can happen
under these circumstances?

In each case, their absence clearly resulted in problems involving
their youngsters. Yet when I asked them what they believed was the
significance of their absence from home, they seemed confused by
the question. They honestly believed they were doing their job.
They blamed the child, the mother or the school. They never considered their own absence.

Gay: There are several problems associated with financial support. First,
in our culture men have made and continue to make more money
than women even when their jobs are the same. Because of this, we
usually see men as the primary breadwinners for the family. This is
true even when both parents work and are capable of earning
about equal pay.

Most contemporary families need dual incomes. But most parents continue to believe that their children need the supervision
and care of at least one parent. I see more and more husbands and
wives jointly deciding to let Mom be the parent and Dad the wage
earner. As a logistical necessity, it seems like the most sensible
option.

The problem is that the decision creates a type of absentee dad.
Not only do the fathers concentrate most of their energies on their

careers, but their wives, as an unspoken part of the agreement, take on the dual role of mother and father.

Predictably, problems within the family begin to crop up as time goes by. Some of these problems demand that both mom and dad play active parenting roles. At times like these many fathers find that they are trapped outside the family circle. They have agreed to heavy work loads, they travel weekly and frankly, they do not really know what is going on with their kids. In some cases, their efforts to make a difference are resented by everyone. These situations do not make happy endings and, regrettably, I am seeing more and more of them.

Many fathers find that they are trapped outside the family circle.

These types of decisions reflect and verify beliefs about the non crucial contributions men are seen to make with their children. Many women today carry these beliefs even further. For example, I have met some young mothers whose fathers were absent during their early lives. Most were raised by their mothers because of divorce, but others had emotionally absent fathers.

These women completely discount the role of fathers. Perhaps because they did not experience having a father, they have decided that raising a child does not require a father at all. Most have never considered the issues thoroughly. All they know is they want a baby of their own.

There has been an upswing in the numbers of middle class, single women who have chosen to become mothers without husbands. Consider this: single mothers spend a third less time with their children than do working mothers. This means that the children will spend more time being raised by other people. This fact alone has major implications, but the permanent factor seems to hinge on the devaluation of the father's role. I find all this very frightening for children.

Ron: So the issue of financial support boils down to not who can make more money, but shared belief that if dad spends time away from home earning money, then there is nothing to worry about as long as mom is available to the children. This belief completely overlooks the complementary role fathers play in the lives of their kids. Many mothers and fathers make parenting decisions based on the assumption that there needs to be at least one parent, and mom is enough. This notion is not only incorrect, it's stupid. As Gay has pointed out, some women with higher earnings have concluded that they do not need men at all to raise a kid. It is true that women may not need husbands, but children continue to need fathers!

So Gay, what's a mother to do?

Gay: I believe moms and dads have to include the needs of their children when making financial decisions. Children need what fathers have to offer. Children with fathers who are present and active turn out better than kids who do not. The evidence is everywhere. It's common sense.

It does not make sense in the long run for parents to adopt lifestyles that intentionally put Dad on the outside looking in at his kids. If a raise in pay means that Dad would spend significantly less time at home, the family needs to rethink their priorities. Dads need to be home and mothers need to encourage dads to stay connected with their kids.

Women may not need husbands, but children need fathers!

CAREGIVING

Ron: There are two points I want to make about masculine caregiving. First, truly effective dads see themselves as caregivers. They begin caregiving early in the child's life. I have learned that fathers approach caregiving from a much different perspective than moms. For example, the fathers seem not to associate caregiving with their personal identity. They view caregiving tasks in much the same way they think about changing the oil of the car or getting the blades sharpened on the lawnmower. We need to care for things that we value. It's just that simple! If you love your children, you take care of them. What's the big deal?

Second, there is a unique characteristic of effective dads. They teach their child to care for themselves. They view caregiving as a way to emphasize the necessity for the child to take care of himself or herself. That's a different perspective on caregiving from that of mothers.

However, in our American culture, caregiving is not associated with masculinity. As a consequence, major obstacles that some fathers must overcome are the lame-brain rules about what men do and do not do.

Such rules are powerful but do not make any sense. Men play caregiving roles at many levels of our society. Ranchers and farmers take care of their animals. Male physicians and physical therapists care for patients. I am a psychologist. We are all caregivers. The whole notion that there is men's work and women's work associated with child rearing is archaic.

I will tell you something else. Just because men believe these things does not mean women do not believe them as well. For example, one of the prime caregiving obstacles fathers encounter when attempting to participate in caring for their child is being blocked by their kid's mom.

How does that fit with your experience Gay?

One of the prime care-giving obstacles fathers encounter is being blocked by their kid's mom.

Gay: The number one problem is that moms view it as their job to be the primary caregiver. We have learned from our mothers and grandmothers that this is our role exclusively. So when men move in and attempt to take more active roles, we feel threatened.

On one hand, women might say, "It's about time. I need the help." On the other hand, most women think that men do not do a very good job. They do not "do" caregiving like women "do" it. Women ask for help from their husbands, but are often critical because the tasks are not being done the same way they want them done.

Women typically believe things should be done our way. We believe it is our role to protect, care for and nurture. Frequently we incite conflict because our husband wants to make the kids do more for themselves. We moms want to keep our role because it is a major source of our identity.

I agree that moms are often gatekeepers. They want to make sure their children stay safe. If they see Dad's way of caregiving as reckless and without apparent thought to the child's comfort, they will intervene.

Ron: I have learned a great deal from working class mothers and dads that has influenced my thinking about masculine caregiving. Sometimes these mothers and fathers work different shifts. In these cases, the fathers just naturally take on all the caregiving activities typically associated with women. Necessity dictates that both parents share caregiving tasks. In these situations, the issue of the father's incompetence disappears completely. Remember the research we discussed earlier. Those findings indicated that after the baby's first year, mothers are far more competent, than are dads, at caregiving. These working class men and women provide notable exceptions to these findings. When dads and moms simply must share caregiving responsibilities, men learn these skills rapidly and well. The masculinity issue never arises at all.

In my way of thinking, caregiving is the doorway through which dads must walk to connect with their child. The child grows to sense that the father cares for, loves and will protect her/him. Caregiving also allows the mother an opportunity to observe the father caring for the child.

Caregiving allows the father to earn the mother's trust. This is essential. The father needs to earn the mom's trust that he will not harm her child. It is an issue of competence. This trust allows her to support other parts of his job later in the child's life.

So what's a mom to do, Gay?

Caregiving allows the father to earn the mother's trust.

Gay: Moms need to acknowledge that their children need the connection with their dads. At times, moms must be willing teachers in order to raise dads' level of caregiving competence. At the same time moms need to recognize that once Dad has the skills, she needs to step back and allow Dad to do things his way. Allow flexibility.

Now many of we mothers have difficulty letting go of our control. By keeping the control we feel we can guarantee our children's safety. In my workshops, I talk with a lot of moms about allowing dads more opportunities to provide caregiving. In fact, many moms agree that the biggest obstacles to dads being more involved, is their discomfort at standing back and allowing dads to make mistakes. And yet, when moms are able to relax, they report definite positive benefits when children and their fathers are connected.

TRUST

Ron: A key role of dads is to prepare their children for life outside the security of the home. One of the skills we are required to know is how to form trusting relationships. When we form relationships we sometimes mistakenly assume that if we invest trust in others, we can automatically trust them in return. This assumption of automatic trust introduces many of us to an undeniable factor of real life...betrayal. When we trust others, our relationships carry the potential for betrayal. Trust and betrayal are two sides of the same coin.

Trust and betrayal are two sides of the same coin.

Dads teach trust to their youngsters by modeling. A father models how men show respect for women through the ways he behaves with the child's mother. Father teaches about trusting outsiders through the unspoken relationship that he develops with his child.

The respected psychologist, James Hillman, has written that the trust between the mother and the child is biologically established. The mother comes prepared to nourish the child from her body. The relationship of trust between the mother and child is sustained by the child's dependence upon the mother. This dependent relationship is one in which the child seeks safety, comfort, and protection from the mother. The dependent nature of this relationship is sustained long after the child is no longer nursing.

The father forges the contract of trust based on his "word."

The bond of trust between the father and the child is not biological. It is more like a binding contract in which the father earns the child's trust. In essence, the father forges the contract of trust based on his "word." The child's trust is sustained when the father keeps his commitments. So the father-child relationship becomes the model or template for all trusting relationships other than the mother.

However, it is impossible for any of us to honor every commitment. So dads fail. When fathers fail to keep their word, they introduce their children to betrayal. In some cases, such as not attending a play, the betrayal is not so great. In other instances, those in which fathers are separated from and abandon their children by divorce or when men are abusive, the betrayal is much deeper.

Success in life demands that we understand the relationship between trust and betrayal. It is essential. Children without fathers often do not know who to trust. They stay dependent upon their mother. These children yearn to trust others and yet struggle with the issues of betrayal. They do not know when to trust others and when it's best to trust in oneself.

Gay, what's a mother's perspective?

Gay: Fathers are the first and most powerful *significant other.* Children need to have trusting relationships with their father. And yet, one of the most consistent issues raised by women in therapy and by mothers is that women perceive that men do not keep their word to them or to their children. Instead, they associate men with broken promises–betrayal.

When women mistrust their husbands, they become more protective and more controlling in order to insure that their children feel safe. Mothers want their children to know that the kids can depend on mom at least. Sometimes, moms who have been abandoned by their fathers do not want to give Dad a chance. They become locked in by their own fears of mistrust. They identify the children as "my children" as opposed to "our children." They become more controlling and less flexible. These mothers openly blame the father for his shortcomings in front of the children. These situations teach children to mistrust others in general and men in particular.

Ron: All trusting relationships carry the potential for betrayal. When dads live up to their promises and keep their commitments, they portray for the child a model of a person who can be trusted. In essence, the father's behavior says, "If you're going to trust someone, trust someone who behaves like I do." As a child grows older, effective dads gain the power to teach their children to trust their own judgment and stand independently.

However, untrustworthy fathers introduce their youngsters to betrayal. Unable to establish a trusting relationship with the father, children have a difficult time entering relationships with anyone other than their mother. They choose companions poorly. Often these relationships are bitterly disappointing.

So what's a mom to do, Gay?

Gay: I think trust issues are the most complex that we face. What a mom needs to do is to communicate more clearly with her husband about the things he is doing that make it difficult to trust him. Give Dad the chance to make commitments and to keep them. Remember, the goal is to teach kids how to form trusting relationships. The goal is not to teach kids they can't trust anyone, especially men.

Remember, the goal is not to teach kids they can't trust anyone, especially men.

There is one other issue. Some women need to look at their own past relationships with significant men in their lives. They need to determine if their mistrust of their husband is really associated with their husband right now, or more accurately, a reflection of their mistrust of men based on their personal experiences with their fathers. It's essential that they stay clear about where the blame lies. If there is a problem with the mother's perspective, it needs to be addressed.

IDENTITY

Ron: Let's talk about the father's role in the formation of his child's identity. Child development specialists tell us that, at birth, children do not perceive themselves as separate persons from their mother. It is a challenge for the child to achieve a separate identity from the mother. Being able to see ourselves as individuals with our own interests, goals and ways of solving problems is essential. One of the roles of the father is to assist the child with this process.

The father is the "significant other" in the child's life. When the dad enters the picture, the child is provided with contrasting points of view, values and ways of approaching life from those of the mother. Mothers are not men, and fathers are not women. They view life differently. And in the formation of their personal identity, the child benefits from this contrast.

Children are continuous observers. They learn about men and women, and about relationships, by watching how their parents deal with problems in different ways. They watch the give and take of their parents relationship; and the balance of power shifting between the mother and father.

The child absorbs these things and a unique self awareness begins to emerge. This new self is a combination of both the mother and the father. Encoded within the child are the perceptions, pictures and words of both the father and mother. From this combination, a unique personality emerges which is a conglomerate of both mom and dad. It is a dynamic process.

The critical problem associated with identity is the absentee dad.

The critical problem associated with the formation of identity is the absentee dad. When dads are absent, this process of identity formation is thrown out of balance. The child has input primarily from the mom. Without the contrast provided by the father, the struggle to become autonomous from the mother becomes far more difficult.

Gay: Both girl and boy children learn about men and women through having both Mom and Dad present. Obviously, moms cannot be dads. Women's growing up experiences are very different from the way men are brought up. We may share much, with the opposite sex but our perspectives are different. Children need the contrast between dads' and moms' perceptions in order to get a balanced picture.

88

It is no less important for girls to be around their dads than it is for boys. Girls learn from their dad's presence what husbands do, how moms and dads solve problems or how to be in a committed relationship. The problem is that frequently dads discount their role with their female children. It has been my experience that dads have played a significant role in women's lives. Fathers influence their daughters either by their positive presence or by their absence. Women suffer by not having the experience of learning what men do and how men think.

The critical issue is Mom's lack of awareness of the problems that happen when Dad is not there. Many women fail to realize while they can provide income, nurturing and a role model for what women do, they cannot be men. They cannot be substitute fathers.

Ron: The issue of absentee fathers becomes critical when discussing identity formation. Dad's influence is essential. Dad does not have to have super powers, be perfect or ultra masculine. However, dads must be available to their children and aware of their influence as teachers.

Children observe everything. They observe how Mom and Dad get along together, they observe when they do not get along together. They learn, whether we want them to or not, how to make relationships work or not work. This form of learning goes on automatically and it is exceedingly powerful. Kids observe and learn from both the positive and negative aspects of relationships as well.

Dad can be a wonderful human being. He can be handsome, rich, humorous and a great athlete. But, if he is also absent, then girls learn that husbands are wonderful and absent. Boys learn that dads come home now and then, act like Mr. Know-It-All, and disappear. That's exactly the way they will expect their relationships to be like in the future.

It is important for dads to understand that they have an important job to do at home. To do this job, they have to be with their children. It does not matter to the child if Dad's job demands that they travel all the time. When men become fathers, they are obligated to reexamine their priorities.

So Gay?

When men become fathers, they are obligated to reexamine their priorities.

Gay: Moms need to be aware of these issues. They need to encourage the father to be there; to be involved. When Mom and Dad discuss job changes for him, or career opportunities he might pursue, they have to put these issues in balance. They have to be careful to explore their decisions. Everyone believes that they need more money. We want good things for our families. But Mom must realize all the money in the world is not going to allow children to learn what they need to know from their father if Dad is unavailable.

I see married and single women who have children and discount the fathers' role. When children are brought up exclusively by the mother, the children are much less likely to be successful forming healthy relationships; they lack independence and self confidence.

FAMILY TRADITIONS

Traditions provide an excellent way for dads to reconnect with their youngsters.

Ron: Traditions provide an excellent way for dads to reconnect with their youngsters. Not only do traditions reconnect father with their kids, but traditions also provide a continuity for the child within their family's history. Traditions allow kids to become part of things that have gone on in the past. Traditions allow fathers and their children to form a special identity that is a legacy that the child carries into adulthood.

Unlike the typical family tradition, I have discovered that the traditions that dads create are often unrelated to religious observances. Instead, they are more often a reflection of things dads enjoy intensely. Whether it's the first day of baseball season, going on the yearly camping trip or gathering firewood in the fall, these are things that dads love doing and personally identify with.

When dads share their passion for life with their children by insuring that their kids participate, the connection is established. Traditions are powerful, easy to establish and regrettably, too often overlooked.

Gay, what do you think?

Gay: I agree with you. Traditions are important. Traditions help kids feel safe. Things that we do that are predictable in nature, whether it's celebrating birthdays or going camping or hiking makes kids feel secure. And they add to that identity we just talked about.

I remember that my dad traveled a lot. On Sundays, mom got breakfast in bed. First, Dad and we kids made her breakfast. Then

Dad made pancakes for us. That was a pretty important way for us to spend time alone with Dad.

I think moms play an important role in the more typical traditions that help with family connectiveness, birthday celebrations, religious holiday celebrations, etc. As kids and their parents are involved in the traditions, there is a greater sense of connectiveness and continuity. I think it helps contribute to the kids' feeling of safety.

Ron: Traditions often seem to spring "out of the blue." That spontaneity is one of the things that makes them so powerful. If going rafting down a river is the high point of the vacation, rafting might be repeated year after year. The important thing is that traditions work because they glue family members together in some activity that everybody seems to enjoy.

Traditions work because they glue family members together.

I have discovered that a lot of kids do not know very much about their fathers. Well, traditions provide kids with ways to step into the lives of their fathers. They help kids learn about their father.

So what's a mom to do, Gay?

Gay: I recommend that Mom support Dad being involved with their kids by doing some of the things that are traditional for Dad's family. Likewise, mom needs to share with Dad the traditions that were important in her family. By incorporating both sets of traditions, you create a richness that supports the kids feeling of safety and of being connected.

SECURITY

Ron: Security is essential for all families. Typically, security is associated with keeping the family safe from outside intruders. Security means protection from people who want to harm our family members or take our belongings. But I would like to focus our discussion on the internal security within the family.

Effective fathers understand the need to exercise self control over angry and reactive impulses.

Nothing of lasting value can happen inside a family if there is not a genuine sense of safety within it. This means that family members have to respect each other's boundaries. By boundaries, I mean our bodies, possessions, self esteem, emotions and ideas. In the past, fathers have been identified as sometimes brutal individuals who threaten the physical and emotional safety of their own family members.

In contrast, effective fathers understand the need to exercise self control over angry and reactive impulses. By controlling their behavior, such fathers model how their children are to behave.

From another perspective, one of the greatest sources of a child's security is provided by having clear limits on their behavior. When children do not have firm limits, or when limits are inconsistently applied, children will push to find out exactly where their boundaries are. When children know their limits, they are more comfortable within their families. Without boundaries, there is continuous trouble.

There is a potential point of conflict here between mothers and fathers. Dads are more likely to enforce limits with negative consequences. In some instances, fathers' use of punishment to enforce limits becomes a problem for mothers. In the past, fathers have reported that when they have attempted to enforce rules, they have found themselves in conflict with their wife. These fathers reported that their wives responded to them as someone who intended to harm her children. From these fathers' perspectives, mothers often appear better at making rules than enforcing them.

Gay: Security for children is very important. Many mothers have problems with the limits that dads set. We may view the limits as excessively harsh and we do not want our children to be unhappy. Also, moms want to stay connected with their children. In an effort to stay connected, we want the children to understand why what they did was incorrect.

We spend a lot of time explaining things. We try to get our kids to understand why it is important to behave well because they are connected to us. We believe that if the children see it our way, there will be less conflict and fewer problems. We do not like conflict and so we try to use reason. In the end, we give them one more chance. Frequently, all this explaining causes conflict with the kids' dad who gets weary of listening to discussions and negotiations between mom and the children without any change in behavior.

Ron: When moms and dads are not in agreement about how to deal with discipline issues, the kids recognize their conflict very rapidly. As a consequence, kids learn to profit from Dad and Mom's conflict by adopting a tactic called "splitting." Splitting occurs when the kids recognize when dads and moms do not agree on how discipline issues are to be resolved. Splitting is a form of parental manipulation in which kids play moms off dads and dads off moms. Every parent is familiar with this pattern of behavior. Chances are you used it on your folks when you were a kid. It works particularly well if Mom or Dad is over reactive. If Mom and Dad quarrel often and angrily, it tends to polarize and crystallize their positions. This situation is great for kids since it makes splitting easier with each passing explosion.

Splitting is a form of parental manipulation in which kids play moms off dads and dads off moms.

Splitting does not mean the kids are bad. What it means is that they are perceptive, bright kids whose parents are ineffective. These situations grow worse over time. Moms and dads argue more and more and the kids' behavior gets more disruptive. Children need to learn how to behave themselves.

Take it, Gay.

Gay: I think that both parents need to set limits for their children. It's important to establish rules and consequences before children get themselves into trouble. For example, in our practice, we often use contracts that clearly specify expectations as well as the consequences if those expectations are not met.

Ironing out contracts ahead of time assures that the provisions set down are agreeable to both parents. This eliminates dissension and allows parents to minimize splitting. By planning ahead, Mom and Dad can eliminate misunderstanding down the line. Limits create a sense of security for the youngster that comes from being able to predict the outcomes of their behavior.

Limits create a sense of security that comes from being able to predict the outcomes.

SELF PROTECTION

Ron: Life is tough and it's not getting any easier. Regardless of our education, occupation or income level, we have to be prepared to take care of ourselves. Self protection means protecting our boundaries. As we discussed, our boundaries refer to our physical bodies, possessions, emotions, ideas and accomplishments. Typically, when people think of self protection, they tend to think about the types of skills men are taught to defend themselves. But it is equally important for girls to be prepared to defend themselves and their possessions.

We cannot talk about defending our boundaries without considering the issue of anxiety. Typically if we are threatened, the experience triggers anxiety. Now, moms view themselves as protectors. It is an important part of their job to protect and to keep the child safe from injury and discomfort. This is an essential role when children are very young.

However, life demands that children know how to protect themselves when Mom is no longer available. Moms cannot follow their children into adult life. The youngster must learn to protect him or herself. While mothers urge children to avoid threatening situations, dads through adventure and play pull their youngster into situations that increasingly demand and teach self protection.

Gay: The problem with fathers teaching self protection is that it is very difficult for moms to not feel our stomachs tie in knots when our children do things that we see as risky.

Our son takes martial arts. Once a mom told me that she will never attend her son's belt tests because she cannot handle watching her child sparring, even though the children are heavily protected. Despite all the obvious safety precautions, the mother found it too uncomfortable to watch her child participate in a combative situation. Women want their children to be safe. We tend to want to be certain that no harm comes to them. Most of us encourage our kids to take fewer risks than their father.

Ron: Dads and moms play complementary roles. Dad encourages the youngster to take calculated risks and the mom encourages the child to use caution and avoid unnecessary or impulsive risk taking. Later in life the balance of the mother's and father's influence can be seen in the workplace and in other relationships that can involve conflict and, at times, a violation of our personal boundaries.

When our boundaries have been threatened, the masculine model is to be aggressive, for example, to litigate: hire the smartest, mad dog attorney and sue the rascals. Often this approach leaves the situation in a complete state of shambles. The mothers' approach to self protection might not involve litigation.

Gay, what can mothers to do to help a child be self protective?

Gay: There is no doubt that even though self protection issues may trig-

94

ger our anxiety, mothers must acknowledge that it is necessary for children to learn to take care of themselves. But self protective does not necessarily mean combative. I believe that mediation is a form of self protection that is less combative, for example, than litigation.

Self protective does not necessarily mean combative.

Mediation skills can be taught to elementary school aged children and practiced in our homes. In a related way, both mothers and fathers can teach and encourage their children to become assertive. Children need to be able to say what they really want, and to say "no" as well. I have found that while moms agree that it is important for their kids to say no to others, it's not always comfortable to have them say no to Mom. And that's where mediation skills become useful.

If mothers do not feel safe allowing certain types of activities, then it's important to stop the action before it begins. By discussing her concerns, it is possible to identify what conditions could be changed to allow her safety issues to be satisfied. For example, many parents make it a point to meet and talk with the parents of their children's friends. Later in the child's life, parents and kids work out contracts that prohibit drinking and driving.

Finally, mothers and dads must have a trusting relationship regarding the child's safety. When Mom knows that her partner is equally concerned about their child's well being, then it is easier for her to accept the risk taking behavior necessary for kids to be successful in the real world.

HUMOR

Ron: Humor serves two purposes. First, humor combined with play creates a magnet that draws kids and fathers together. The work of children is play. A child's reality is defined by play. When dads enter into the child's world through laughter and play, it allows the father to gain power as a teacher and role model. And this teaching role is related to the second purpose of humor.

Play creates a magnet that draws kids and fathers together.

In the distant past, the role of the jester was aimed at reminding us that our beliefs and assumptions about reality can betray us. Real life plays by its own rules. Life is not fair and at times it is frightening. The real world is unforgiving and its lessons are often harsh.

Children need to learn about real life and yet no parent wants to overwhelm or frighten their child. Humor is a natural way to reduce anxiety. As fathers emphasize their children's competence through competition, anxiety is a typical by-product. Humor dispels performance related anxiety. It reduces tension and allows the child to relax, learn and perform.

In some instances the father's humor may seem cruel or obscene. But then so is life and so was the court jester. The ability to laugh when we are anxious is an essential skill that helps the child integrate herself/himself into reality. Gay?

Gay: Well, moms use humor, but moms use humor differently. Moms tend to use humor to try to reduce anger when there have been problems within the family. Moms use humor to reestablish family harmony. Moms do not like angry children. They do not like to feel distant from their children. Humor is an attempt to reestablish the connection.

The problems moms have with dads' use of humor arise because dads tend to use humor to exaggerate and make fun of seemingly serious situations. Sometimes men make fun of other people and other cultures. At times moms say that fathers are too silly. They do not take life seriously enough. A mom may berate her husband for using humor when she views its use as inappropriate. It is almost as if men's humor borders on being too wild; too uncontrolled for safety.

Anxiety and anger are two sides of the same coin.

Ron: Humor is a powerful tool for both moms and dads. Humor seems linked to dealing with our feelings of anxiety and anger. Anxiety and anger are two sides of the same coin. Both are triggered by threatening situations. Dads use humor to reduce anxiety when introducing the kid to real life situations. Moms use humor to reduce anger within the family.

And, she said....

Gay: Well, I think that Mom needs to recognize the different ways in which humor is used by men and women. If she is feeling particularly concerned about the father's approach, then set aside time to discuss the issues and her feelings about them. Also, work to insure that the children understand the values that both Mom and Dad believe are important, for example, respect for other people.

COURAGE

Ron: When we think about courage, probably most of us recall heroic acts we have seen portrayed in newspapers or on TV. Some of these memories probably include those of individuals who have rescued others from dangerous situations or people who have lived through life threatening events through personal courage. This type of courage is not what I am talking about.

The type of courage that I want to discuss has two elements. The first is sometimes known as perseverance. At some time, all of us will encounter situations in which we are confronted by adversity. These situations may seem beyond our control. And yet through personal courageousness, we remain self protective and maintain our sense of integrity. Examples include individuals who have overcome failure, rejection, physical disabilities and prejudice.

Through personal courageousness, we remain self protective and maintain our integrity.

The second type of courage is portrayed when we are willing to accept life's challenges by taking calculated risks. Throughout life, we sometimes find ourselves at crossroads. By crossroads, I mean challenges. Will we choose to live life in a safe, yet unfulfilling way, or will we accept our challenges, endure anxiety, become competent and move toward an expansion of our sense of awareness and level of performance.

This form of courage has been portrayed by men and women throughout history. This willingness to test ourselves is taught through adventure and pushing our limits. Dads greatly contribute to the development of perseverance and the willingness to take calculated risks.

Gay: Women and men teach courage. However, the problem that mothers have with the risks that fathers encourage is that the risks are too big. We moms do not like to see our children fail. Frequently, we may find ourselves in conflict with our husband about these issues. Dad will be pushing hard and Mom will feel that things need to go slower, more cautiously.

We want our children to excel. We also seem to feel our children's anxiety at greater depths than do our husbands.

When mothers sense their children's anxiety, their first impulse is to pull them out of the situation—to be protective. However, women also recognize that they have to encourage and push, so there is an inner conflict within the mom about how much to push and how much to protect. When she is confused about these issues, sometimes her inner turmoil will trigger conflict between her and the kids' dad.

When dads encourage youngsters to take risks and moms protect the youngster, conflict is predictable.

Ron: You are right. When dads encourage youngsters to take risks and moms do their job to protect the youngster, conflict is predictable. I honestly believe that this form of conflict can be healthy. The conflict teaches kids that both mom and dad view their responsibilities importantly. The conflict demonstrates that both parents care enough about the kids that they are willing to defend their beliefs. This is good.

Some people seem to think that children should not see their parents quarrel. In this instance, however, I believe it is actually beneficial for youngsters to witness both parents standing up for their beliefs about what is best for the child. Sometimes moms do know best; and, at other times, Dad may be justified. The kid is the real winner.

In fact, there is something that bothers me about many of today's young fathers. When their wives get angry about these issues, the dads cave in. They run from their wife's anger. By failing to confront the issues, they demonstrate that courage is just something that dads talk about, but that dads do not really act courageously. In those instances, fathers betray their youngsters by not doing their job.

Gay?

Gay: Conflict is going to occur between Mom and Dad and risks are necessary. Children do not learn to be courageous without taking risks. I encourage compromise and negotiation. Get to an understanding about why Dad is encouraging the risk-taking behavior. What are the benefits that Dad sees. Recognize that it may take self control to be able to contain the rising anxiety within the mother. The child may not be experiencing anxiety at all! Sometimes the support of other women in discussing these issues is helpful.

INDEPENDENCE

Ron: To talk about independence, let's go back to our discussion of caregiving. Caregivers are essential to children and mothers play a primary role in caregiving. Their natural orientation is directed

98

toward caregiving and there is much to learn from moms in this regard. But it is important to understand that there is a shadow side to caregiving.

The negative side of caregiving is dependence. When there is an over emphasis on caregiving, youngsters become overly dependent. I have interviewed dozens of "stay-at-home" moms. They defined "being a good mom" as doing everything for their child. On the surface this appears to be a loving attitude toward parenting, but the dependency it creates is not tolerated by the real world. *The negative side of caregiving is dependence.*

Individuals who are not independent, who are not prepared to stand on their own and do things for themselves, rapidly discover that the real world has no place for them.

This is an issue where women and men's perspectives can differ widely. The dads' rule of thumb is: Don't do for the child what the child can do for himself. The moms' rule is just the opposite. That is, good moms do everything for their children.

Gay: The problem is that moms often extend our role as caretaker to ensuring that the child stays comfortable and has his/her needs met. Moms gain a lot of our identity from being caregivers. Intellectually, we know that the child has to be independent. On the other hand, moms become uncomfortable with the distancing that occurs with independence. Moms want to be needed. As her child needs her less, mom begins to question her role and their identity. She feels anxiety. Dependent children are tolerated, of course, because their dependence sustains the relationship and verifies Mom's identity as primary caregiver. However, the sustained dependence on the mother makes it difficult for the youngster to learn to care for him/herself when the time comes to be on their own.

Ron: One of the most difficult situations we encounter is that of college-aged kids who are totally unprepared to live away from home. In many instances, the females never leave home or they become pregnant. Male underachievers fail miserably at nearly everything and drop out. These youngsters are bright and they are capable of making the transition. The problem is that they have been cared for like large pets. I believe that it is dads' intolerance of dependence that propels kids toward the development of the competencies needed to succeed as adults. *Dads' intolerance of dependence propels kid's toward the development of the competencies needed to succeed.*

Female children who have active dads are more ambitious. They attend and complete college work. They choose careers that allow them to provide for themselves. This goes for male children as well. Ambition is a characteristic of children raised in families where dads emphasize independence and self reliance.

Gay: These issues are particularly difficult for single mothers and mothers married to absentee husbands. Moms should support dads' efforts to spend time along with their kids. Fathers who take their children to work, initiate work projects around the home and help kids with homework teach self reliance.

I encourage moms to set personal goals for themselves that redefine their roles once the kids are older. Many women have found that both they and their children profit when Mom recreates her identity in non-caregiving ways. Often this is accomplished by allowing Dad to play an increasingly broadened role as they re-focus their attention on themselves.

The transition away from caregiving is probably a greater struggle for the mother than the children. Kids attending schools soon learn that teachers are much less accommodating than most mothers. The kids learn quickly, but moms may have more trouble giving up their role and adopting new attitudes. Dads can help if moms are willing to listen.

SELF CONFIDENCE

Ron: Life demands that we learn from our mistakes. We have to be able to learn rapidly. By self confidence I mean a sense of trust we have in our ability to succeed.

Learning self confidence cannot occur without mistakes.

Self confidence is taught. It is gained when we see that there is a relationship between what we do and what happens to us as a consequence. Learning self confidence cannot occur without mistakes. In essence, the child has to experience some level of failure to learn to be self-corrective and to persevere. That way, when our kids have new experiences in the future, even if success is not immediate, they will have a sense of self trust that will allow them to continue through the rough period and ultimately succeed.

Self confidence allows us to stay connected with what we are working on even though it is difficult. It is essential. Fathers teach self confidence by encouraging their youngsters. However, when

100

fathers overly identify with the success of their child, they become critical. They become perfectionists. Critical fathers damage their children's self confidence. A difficult task for many dads is to contain their criticism. And yet, teaching youngsters to be self confident demands that fathers learn self control.

Gay: The moms' role in teaching self confidence is really not that different from those of the dads. The problem is that it is difficult for mothers to allow their child to experience failure. Frequently moms rush in and pull their kids out of situations that the child appears to be in over their head. Mothers will say, "It's OK if you drop out of this one. You don't have to do this. It's too hard. You're not ready." When moms do this, it might be acting out of concern for the child and her fear that the child's self esteem is going to be damaged. In fact, it backfires! When moms rescue their kids from difficult situations, it teaches the children, "You're right, you can't do this, you're not capable. You're not competent." By rescuing, she is doing exactly the opposite of what she really wishes to do, which is to build the child's self esteem. She is teaching them to solve difficult problems by avoiding them.

Ron: So let's say that the mom is willing to bite the bullet and allow her kid to experience difficult situations. We still cannot escape from the fact that fathers can kill the self confidence in the child by being overly critical. I have found that for many dads, resolving their criticism requires building a contract between the father and child. The father is allowed to coach the kid during practice, but when it comes time for the big game, the dad agrees to keep quiet except for cheering. Children want their dads to watch them compete. But at game time, dads have to put a sock in it, tape their mouth shut or whatever it requires to contain their criticism. If they criticize the child, it kills their self confidence.

Fathers can kill the self confidence in the child by being overly critical.

Gay: Moms, who recognize that their husband is overly critical, need to set up a contract with dad. Find a way that is not embarrassing to rein in his criticism. When they attend an event at which Dad is getting carried away with criticism, he needs to go into "time out."

This can be difficult. Moms and dads frequently get into conflict because moms view dads as overly pushy and dads view moms as not wanting the child to do his/her very best. Perhaps the contract might be between Dad and the kids and Mom. Both Mom and Dad keep their commitment to each other and the kids are committed also.

PATIENCE

Ron: Patience is difficult for many fathers to master. Real life demands that we become skilled. There is no way around it. We have to be competent to be successful. Becoming competent requires new experiences and with each new experience comes the possibility for making mistakes.

When mistakes are paired with the father's angry impatience, the youngster responds by becoming either frightened or angry at the father. In either case the anxiety and anger distract the child. It switches the kids' focus away from learning and towards their feelings. This loss of focus retards learning and actually increases the number of mistakes.

Becoming patient requires that the father look within himself. Fathers need to recognize that the need to be a perfect father unrealistically demands that his children remain perfect as well. We know our children have to be skilled, and so a father cannot just say, "Well, this is just the way I am." This may be really tough, but dads must realize...impatience sustains incompetence.

Impatience sustains incompetence.

Gay: This is an arena in which men and women are more alike than they are different. I think we moms have difficulty modeling the patience we want our children to have.

It is difficult to be patient in a world where things move as fast as they do. There seem to be demands on everyone's time. We are required to do things quickly and to do them accurately. There does not seem to be much room for error. And yet, when moms and dads display impatience, it is difficult for children not to be impatient.

Perseverance is learned when disappointing life events are paired with patience.

Ron: Perseverance is learned when disappointing life events are paired with patience. Parents teach perseverance when they say, "Look, we'll hang in there with you. It's important that you to do a better job; and we're going to do our part to help you." Part of the job is to avoid becoming infuriated by less-than-perfect performance. Kids learn to persevere—they learn to stay connected with disappointing situations—when their parents are patient teachers.

A lot of people have difficulty responding to their kid's mistakes. Consider this: One of the things that skilled classroom teachers have taught us is that the most powerful form of learning is *corrective feedback*. Corrective feedback is powerful because the teacher uses the learner's mistakes to fine tune his/her understanding of a concept. It's like adjusting how a batter swings the bat by watching what happens when he hits the ball.

Corrective feedback requires two things. First, kids are given permission to make mistakes. The second is that the child values and feels comfortable with the teacher. When parents are impatient, children do not feel comfortable having them as teachers. Instead, the parent makes the child feel anxious. When the parent attempts to correct a mistake, the child becomes distracted and anxious. They fail to learn from their mistakes. Regardless of how important the information might be, the parent's comments are taken as criticism. Impatient parents make learning more difficult.

When parents are impatient, children fail to learn from their mistakes.

Gay: Moms need to recognize the sources of their impatience. It is helpful if Mom and Dad have a signaling system between the two of them that indicates when the other person is losing patience. Frequently when the parent gets in the middle of providing what we believe is wonderful feedback, the child is feeling punished and criticized. The kid becomes less receptive. As the parent senses the child becoming less receptive, they become increasingly less patient. If moms and dads have an agreed upon signal, say during homework time, they can often break the criticism cycle. It is possible to diffuse such situations without being overly critical of Dad or Mom in front of your youngster.

FORGIVENESS

Ron: Forgiveness: There is good news and bad news. First, the bad news. Real life is filled with disappointments. Dealing poorly with life's disappointments is one of the greatest sources of emotional distress and depression that we encounter. So let's look briefly at what happens when we are disappointed. Typically, disappointments trigger anger. Anger seems to trigger blaming, and blaming often leads to circular decision making.

Forgiveness allows us to let go of the anger. It allows people to deal with disappointments in a less distorted way. When we give up our anger, we are able to look at how we contributed to our disappointment without self blame. Containing our anger allows us to accept the reality that sometimes life brings us disappointment. Accepting things as they are allows us to adjust to such events with less distress and to think more clearly. This is the good news.

Dads teach forgiveness by acknowledging their own mistakes and by being willing to ask for their youngsters' forgiveness. That's right. Dads model forgiveness. When dads have been unreasonably impatient, or excessively critical or when they have disappointed their youngster by not honoring a commitment, fathers need to apologize.

Moreover, dads must be willing to forgive their children. It is important to sincerely and genuinely forgive when the child has made a mistake.

It is interesting, as children become adolescents and teenagers, many parents seem betrayed when their children use poor judgment. To a very real extent, however, the teenage years are when kids need permission to make their mistakes. Adolescence is a rehearsal for real life. During this stage, moms and dads are still available to play an important parenting role. Our willingness to forgive our children and help them make better choices in the future is essential. This does not happen unless we parents are willing to forgive. And since dads are often associated with punishment, it is important for dads to understand the need to enforce limits and to forgive our children at the same time.

Gay: Well, dads should not feel they have a corner on being unforgiving. The problem women have is our strong identity with our children. We take our children's mistakes personally. We feel we have failed to do our job and that mistakes are a poor reflection on us as mothers. As our kids get older, they make more mistakes because they are preparing for real life. Moms must understand this process and work with Dad to provide an environment that encourages the kids to do their best and allows them to make mistakes as they stretch to do things they have not done before.

Mom and Dad both need to acknowledge when we make mistakes, and allow our youngsters to see how we parents handle our own mistakes. If Mom and Dad act as if adults do not make mistakes, then our children are betrayed. If the parents teach that everyone makes mistakes and is obligated to resolve them, their kids will learn from their parents' behavior.

Ron: It is important to understand that there are no perfect fathers. As I interviewed hundreds of dads, I have learned that many men seemed genuinely insecure about being good fathers. They were confused and worried. The more we worry about how well we are doing, the more we tend to become perfectionists. Many yearn to be perfect dads. Such aspirations are self defeating.

Think about it. If dads are representative of real life, then we must accept the reality of our imperfection. Real life is not perfect. Real life does not tolerate notions of perfectionism.

Learning to forgive means learning to understand. Understanding teaches self acceptance. Self acceptance is taught when dads portray themselves as real human beings. It is a major mistake when fathers portray ourselves to our children as if we were the best kids in class, did everything our folks told us to do, never made mistakes, and that we were popular and athletic. First, the kids will probably know their old man is full of bologna. In any case, such stories do not do a kid any favors. Our kids need parents like themselves. Kids need real people, who struggle, learn, make mistakes, feel insecure, learn to persevere and eventually gain self confidence, as their role models. Learning to forgive ourselves means accepting that we are not perfect.

Self acceptance is taught when dads portray themselves as real human beings.

Gay: I think that moms and dads who expect perfect children do a disservice to them. Making mistakes is natural. Forgiving ourselves and others is essential. We must clearly communicate to our youngsters, and to husbands as well, that none of us screws up on purpose. Most mistakes are honest. We can learn from our mistakes and do things differently the next time, but typically this does not happen when parents are perfectionists.

CONCLUSION

We are about finished discussing the different and sometimes shared perspectives moms and dads have about their jobs. Being a parent is not easy. Our obligations are always changing and never ending. Because of this, we have attempted to emphasize that kids need the balance of a mother and a father.

And like it or not, if moms and dads both take their job seriously, they are going to experience conflict. Men and women see things from different perspectives and, at times, disagree. This is the way it works. This is where the whole notion of balance comes in. If both parents do their job, then their kids are better prepared to handle real life situations later in life. And this brings us to the subject of adolescents.

So far, the discussion has been directed toward the parents of youngsters from birth to about 10 or 11 years of age. This is a time in which moms and dads have great influence and when both parents must be keenly aware of their mutual obligations.

It has been said that play is the work of children. If that is the case, then adolescence is a rehearsal for real life. When children become adolescents, their focus shifts away from their parents and towards relationships with non-family members. The opportunity for disappointment is much higher. Their lives become far more competitive. Non-family relationships are less accommodating. Adolescents are intolerant of almost any personal flaw. The extent to which parents can successfully give corrective feedback is reduced because of this shift in orientation. Adolescents yearn for independence.

This period brings an increased probability for conflict between adolescents and their mothers. Mothers are often threatened when their youngsters seem intent upon severing their once intimate relationship. Emotions between mother and child often run high during this period. The time has come for the father to step forward and play a more central role.

Regrettably, during this major transition period, many fathers act as if their job is finished. Many abandon their female children entirely and they play a diminished role in the lives of their male children. This is a major mistake. The work is not nearly done. Adolescents still need an active father.

Fathers, as the representatives of the outside world, can play crucial roles in verifying the emerging power and competence of their children. They can also challenge male and female children to see beyond the need to blend with peers to the day when they must stand alone. Fathers help their adolescent children contain surging emotions and channel energy along wholesome paths. And finally, dads come equipped to endure the rejection adolescents typically aim at their parents.

So Who Needs a Father? Our kids, but you knew that already, didn't you?

5

ACCEPT_ing_

the **challenge**

Accepting The Challenge

In this section we will prepare ourselves to make the commitment to become more successful fathers by looking at the elements of change and some of the obstacles we may have to overcome to become the dads our kids need us to be.

ACCEPTING THE CHALLENGE

There are two sides to the fathering issues in our country.

On one side we have found that children with absentee dads run greater risk of being unprepared to handle the challenges of real life. We have also found that active fathers offer essential contributions to their children. When we become aware of these two realities, it brings us to an important decision point.

There is an old saying: When we notice two separate things, we create a third. As it applies to fathering, the third thing is the issue of personal change. It is difficult as a father not to compare ourselves to both absentee and effective dads. This process is called self awareness. The quality of self awareness is an attribute that distinguishes humans from other life forms.

Self Awareness: It cuts both ways. In many cases, when dads learn about the contributions of other fathers, this awareness verifies that they are doing pretty well with their kids. In other cases, dads have reported feelings of distress or even depression.

For some, the comparison of absent dads and active dads produces a sense of being stuck. This feeling combines confusion, dissatisfaction and a slight sense of depression all rolled together. It's associated with the unavoidable sadness that comes when we admit that we are letting our kids down. Maybe we work too much, or have left too much of parenting up to our children's mothers.

Being confused about what to do next is a helpless and uncomfortable situation. In many instances, the complexities confronting fathers who want to be better dads seem almost insurmountable. At times, occupational obligations, relationships ex-wives and lack of confidence in fathering skills trigger an urge for some dads to give up even trying. This is a real dilemma.

WHEN MEN ARE STUMPED

Let's take a look at ourselves. Answer this question. What do men typically do when we do not know what to do?

This is not a meaningless question. There are times in all our lives when the alternatives to not changing are unacceptable and yet the directions for action are unclear. Most of us hate these situations. Like me, most men like to think of themselves as problem solvers. When we cannot come up with workable solutions to our problems, it threatens our sense of competence. In this case, admitting that problems exist at all may seem to reflect poorly on our competence as fathers.

The lessons taught by single custodial fathers make it hard for the rest of us to go to sleep on these issues. None of the single dads I talked with had ever thought that they would be raising their children on their own. For them, not changing their roles as fathers was not an option.

There are times in our lives that demand that we take expert advice. We Americans, both men and women, pay millions of dollars each year for "how to" guidance—expert advice. We go to seminars and counselors; we hire consultants, read books and watch videos. We are starved for solutions.

Let me ask you a question. If the solution to our problems is expert advice, what problems are created by expert solutions? It's important not to miss the point. What do you think are the chances that a sick person, let's say a person with a life threatening disease (like cancer) or maybe faced with potential of blindness, would not follow the advice of a highly qualified medical expert?

Well, if you use your own experiences as a source of information, you will probably recall instances in which you or someone you know did not follow doctor's orders. As it turns out, a sizable percentage of folks who seek expert advice fail to do what experts suggest regardless of how serious or even life threatening the problem may be. A recently published compilation of research studies indicates that between 30% and 80% of

American's fail to follow through on the advice for which we spend our hard earned dollars.

> *In not too distant memory, I spent some time with a man about my own age. The man had been diagnosed with an extremely dangerous type of jaw cancer. Not one, but several, cancer specialists told him that he required an immediate surgical procedure to save his life. The man chose to go through a less reliable form of chemotherapy to the absolute dismay of his doctors. According to my friend, however, his reasons made as much sense as did the experts. Each of the experts, reported the man, gave different odds for his survival. Some set the chances of survival at 65%, while others placed the odds at about 25%.*
>
> *When asked to explain his choice, he told me that he had come to the conclusion that his experts' opinions were slanted in favor of surgery. He believed that the odds they quoted him were aimed at persuading him to agree to the surgery. He remained unconvinced that he would live out a normal life expectancy. A more decisive factor was that after the surgery he would be disfigured. As he put it, "It's hard enough dealing with the idea of dying. If I have to look in the mirror at some sort of freak and still end up dying, I'll take my chances with the chemo."*

This person's experience is repeated dozens of times in equally dramatic and everyday situations as well. For example, when told to use eye drops daily, or go blind, 47% of patients in one study went blind in one eye as a consequence of not using the medication!

At times I find myself saying the same things my father often said to me, "Do something, son, even if it's wrong!" Now that I am grown, I am certain he was trying to teach me that we cannot just sit and try to think our way out of life's problems. There are times when we must risk making mistakes as a way of learning what to do differently to get unstuck.

For now, though, let's take time and use our heads. Let's consider how most of us go about attempting personal change. To begin, let's go backwards in our conversation to the issue of being stuck. What do you think is the typical response men make when they are really stumped? (That is, other than doing nothing.) That's right! They ask someone they believe can give them a straight answer. We are back to expert advice, again. I have learned from experience with dads' support groups that unlike their wives, most fathers absolutely do not equate "sharing problems" with making progress. This is one arena in which men and women are different. The acknowledgment of unsolved problems is not something most men want to share with the guys. If the issue is important enough to talk about, what fathers are looking for is answers. "Just tell me what to do to fix what I'm doing wrong."

You see, there are at least two problems associated with being stumped. One problem is not knowing what to do. The other is knowing what to do, but not wanting to do it! These are important issues for fathers to consider before rushing out for a mega-dose of advice on "how to be a terrific father."

REASONS ABSENTEE DADS GIVE FOR NOT CHANGING

Stick with me here; this is important. I want you to consider the reasons, explanations and justifications most fathers have given for not changing. Look at these:

Reason #1: I don't really want to be a father.

Does this sound familiar? It should, because there are large segments of our male population who are emotionally unprepared to accept the responsibilities of fatherhood. The explanations these guys offer for their unwillingness to become fully engaged with their children reflect a diverse range of reasons. Some are fearful because their own fathers were absent, brutal or drunk, or that they are poor candidates for fathering.

Other men have reported the feelings of betrayal and resentment toward their wives or girlfriends and, in some instances, their own children. These men justify the avoidance of fatherhood because of the anger they harbor at being "tricked" into parenthood by the child's mother. These men report feeling trapped into long term relationships and commitments in which they were not interested.

Many of the fathers of children born out of wedlock and to teenage mothers, as an example, appear unaware that biologically fathering a child implies an opportunity for and obligation to develop a life long relationship with their child. Incidentally, there is strong evidence to suggest that many unwed, teenage mothers share this lack of awareness about the necessity for children to have a father as well.

Considered as a group, men who express these types of reasons may represent the most resistant to personal change. Personal change always starts with both the acknowledgment that change is needed and the acceptance of responsibility to attempt changing ourselves. With angry and frightened men things have to get just about as bad as possible before anything resembling personal change can happen. Most often these guys just disappear.

Reason #2: I don't believe you know what you're talking about.

There are several variations on this theme. For example, many men were raised in households in which their father was deceased, or drunk or always at work. Most often, the men is this group report that they turned out to be hard working family men without a dad to teach them. Other men believe that raising children is women's work and that really masculine males do not do women's work.

There are others as well. Some mothers have reported disbelief that fathers offer unique or irreplaceable contributions that women cannot provide. In most instances, these objections can be resolved by providing a more thorough understanding of what, in many cases, is common sense evidence.

For example, some men have grown up in families without fathers, but have benefited from close relationships with older brothers, uncles and grandfathers. In other instances, single mothers have managed well without the help from anyone. For each of these cases, there are several times as many situations in which the absence of fathers has resulted in negative outcomes. And finally, the lessons taught by single, custodial fathers destroy the myths that raising children is somehow "un-masculine."

Reason #3: I'd like to be a better father, but there are just too many obstacles that get in my way.

Typically, changing our lives boils down to a test of enlightened perseverance. Change–meaningful change–is not easy. Over the years, the most frequently given reasons fathers give for being inactive with their children (even when they live under the same roof) are obstacles that get between them and their kids. For these dads success hinges upon their ability to remove the obstacles that block them from being more active fathers. This where we begin.

SO WHAT ARE THESE OBSTACLES?

There are several areas in which dads encounter obstacles.

Think about your life, about your career and your role in your family. What obstacles do you encounter in staying connected with your children? It is amazing how our lives are so much alike in this regard. Most fathers, much like you and I, report economic obligations and the demands of their job. At a recent workshop, one father responded angrily, "I don't have a choice about how much I work. If I'm not on the job I'll get fired! What control do I have? What can I do?"

> *On one occasion, a man with a troubled expression approached me after one of our sessions. The man told me he had three children ranging from six to seventeen years in age. "I think I'm messing up badly," he began. "I started coming to these talks because my youngest child, my little boy, won't have anything to do with me." I asked him to explain. "Until I came here, I thought I was doing the right thing. I thought there must be something wrong with him. But now, I don't know." I asked what had him confused. "My wife stays at home with the kids. I work three jobs. I have a paper route, my regular job at a computer company and in the evening I'm manager of a pizza place. I'm never home. I've talked to my wife about what I've learned at these talks, but I don't think she's too excited about going back to work."*

In our region of the country, many large corporations tout themselves as "family friendly." In public forums, they point to maternity leave policies as a way of patting themselves on the back. Unfortunately, these benefits seem to be reserved exclusively for women. Fathers I have talked with report that dads who take time off from work to attend teacher conferences or take sick children to the doctor are viewed as "not material for promotion." Some fathers learn to sidestep these invisible barriers by taking personal sick leave to make themselves available when their kids need them. Others have resigned in bitterness from companies who pressed them to place company priorities above those of their children.

Life is difficult, and to a certain extent, so is fathering. What many fathers discover is that their renewed awareness that fathering is essential does not automatically guarantee that their efforts to become active dads will be applauded by the rest of the world. Successful fathering demands a continuous process of weighing the benefits against competing obligations and sources of resistance. At times, the obstacles may be formidable.

Reports from divorced non-custodial and never married teenage fathers reflect a combination of frustration, pain and outrage associated with the limitations imposed on their access to their own children. At times, the combative nature of the process obscures the needs of children for both mothers and fathers.

THE LESSONS OF SINGLE PARENT FATHERS

Once again however, the struggle of single parent fathers provides the rest of us with powerful instructional role models for dealing with obstacles. These men, who make up about 14% of single parents in our country, reflect all races, economic, educational and occupational levels. Their numbers are made up of engineers, meat cutters, guys who load newspapers on trucks and small business owners.

Once they became single fathers, their career, financial and personal priorities changed drastically. Issues such as caregiving, quality time and the need to remove obstacles standing between them and their children demanded immediate and continuous action. These fathers cannot afford the luxury of meaningless debates regarding the masculinity of male parenting. Those of us who are willing to pay attention have much to learn from these fathers.

Now this is important. I have had the opportunity to talk with a great many single parent dads. Among other things, I have learned that these guys are great obstacle removers. Regardless of what their lives may have been like before they became single dads, all of them had to make serious life changes in spite of the same obstacles that the rest of us face. After all single dads still have to work. They have careers and bosses and so on. You get the idea.

Moreover, their success at self change was not initiated by experts. They are *self-changers*. In most cases, these self changers make a lot of mistakes, and they get the job done.

The remarkable thing about these dads is that their failed attempts to become better parents may slow them down, but they do not give up. Now a lot of us view making mistakes as punishment. And everyone knows that we all tend to avoid behaviors that are punished.

Self changers, though, seem to shake off the negative feelings most of us associate with failure. I am not saying these dads do not become frustrated and at times discouraged. They are human and, of course, they experience the same feelings the rest of us do when we screw up. The difference is they do not give up.

Self changers quickly learn what to do, and not do, by doing. Staying stuck is not an option. Incidentally, the term "self changer" has been coined by a team of researchers who set out to discover as much as possible about people who change their lives without the help of experts. Self changers, as it turns out, are everywhere. They lose weight, quit smoking, start new careers and get in shape. Chances are you know someone who has made important changes in their lives.

I talked with a single father who had been raising his son since the boy was about two years old. The dad was an airman in the Air Force when his wife left him and the boy. While in the Air Force, he completed an engineering degree, but discovered that upon graduation, the only available job offerings required that he travel weekly. This dad chose to read electric meters for two years before he found a job that would allow him to be at home with his son.

CHARACTERISTICS OF SELF CHANGERS

Self changers, we have discovered, share many common sense traits that are potentially valuable to those of us interested in playing a greater role in our kids' lives. Consider for example how self changers may deal with their failed attempts. In many cases, self changers may make as many as four or five failed attempts to accomplish their goals.

Think about this. We Americans are about as impatient a crew that can be imagined. We want fast food, easy credit and brief therapy. I have been a family psychologist for a very long time and I do not even have to guess about what would happen if I were to suggest to my clients that they were embarking on a four to five year process. When people seek out experts, they want guaranteed fast results. They want to see rapid progress. No setbacks, thank you very much!

Perhaps because self changers are self reliant, they are forgiving of their setbacks. One feature of their ultimate success, though, is clear. They do make mistakes. In fact, the researchers who have studied these folks tell us that as the number of mistakes increases, so does the probability of their future success! I consider this observation extremely important.

...as the number of mistakes increases, so does the probability of future success!

Not only are self changers flexible, but that there is an active decision making process going on within these folks that directs their behavior. Self changers are not, for example, involved with changing other people. Nor are they dependent upon others to change first in order to allow them to be successful. Instead, they are focused solely on changing themselves.

It seems safe to conclude that self changers, by definition, learn that progress is not related to making the same mistakes over and again. The researchers who interviewed thousands of these individuals have determined that self changers cycle through easily identified stages of change. At the risk of losing you, I am going to list these stages right now. Do not stop reading!

THE STAGES OF CHANGE

In all, the research team has identified five stages that self changers work through. They are:
1. Pre-contemplation (Who cares?) Stage
2. Contemplation (Worry) Stage
3. Preparation (The forgotten) Stage
4. Action (Where did everybody go?) Stage
5. Maintenance (Business as usual) Stage

I am not going to describe all of these stages, but I do want you to look more closely at the middle three: contemplation, preparation and action.

Before going on, however, you need to understand something else about self changers. Self changers essentially do what works. And chances are that they are not unaware that they are cycling through the stages described here. The reason that we are talking about these stages is that they provide a road map for helping us avoid pitfalls and understand what to do when we attempt to make changes and encounter roadblocks.

The Contemplation Stage

The first stage of change that we will consider is the Contemplation Stage. The Contemplation Stage is fancy wording for being worried.

Self changers often stay stuck in the contemplation stage for years. They are aware of the problems, but they are not ready to take action. Many fathers, having learned of the problems children face when their dads are unavailable experience a powerful emotional reaction akin to depression. Fathers in the contemplation stage worry a lot about their kids. They think about possible solutions, but they fear the complexities of changing and the possibility of failure. They are stuck.

Many remain lost in thought. But they gradually begin to shift their focus toward the future. Eventually, the weight of depression gives way to excitement.

As fathers move away from worry and toward the Preparation Stage they find themselves thinking less about the problems and more about doing something about them.

The Preparation Stage

The Preparation Stage is essential, but it is the step most often discounted by self changers.

In my years as a psychologist, I have discovered that most individuals, upon becoming aware of some unsatisfactory aspect of their life, want to change immediately. Critical fathers burn with shame when they realize the paralyzing consequences of their behaviors on their children. They cry and vow to become more supportive, but they fail to consider how they will go about withholding criticism or what they will do instead.

Fathers in the Preparation Stage are committed to action. They are ready to make changes and they say so. Creating a verbal contract or public commitment to action is a key feature of successful self changer efforts.

It is because so many fathers skip this stage that their initial attempts at being better fathers fail. So, it is to this stage that many disappointed fathers must return when they fail to consider that the changes that they intend to make will influence the whole family.

For example, when a young father of a two-year-old reported that he had successfully arranged with his employer to dramatically reduce his out of town travel, he met with unanticipated resistance from his wife. The young mother openly questioned her baffled husband's motives for wanting to be involved in the child's upbringing. She was obviously threatened by his presence and attentiveness to the little girl. As it turned out, the young mother's parents had divorced when she was an infant and she had been raised entirely by her mother and grandmother. The notion of a man holding and caring for a child seemed unfamiliar and somehow unnatural to her.

While this case may seem exaggerated, many men who have initiated more active fathering roles have reported resistance from their wives. This seems to occur especially in homes in which the wife stays home specifically to raise the children.

Recently, I had the opportunity to meet with a moms' support group sponsored by an elementary school. These mothers stayed home, raised the children and managed the household. None held wage earning jobs outside the home. These women viewed themselves as a threatened American sub-population of females. Almost without exception they voiced the belief that "working" mothers, and others, viewed them as dependent, lazy, less valued. Perhaps to combat this image, they defined the roles of mothers as: doing everything for their families, including their husbands.

As a trade off for letting me interview them, I spoke briefly about the contributions of active fathers. Some of the mothers were clearly bothered by what they heard. One woman voiced her concerns by stating that she thought it was her job to see that her husband never had to be "bothered" with the kids. She acknowledged that they had never discussed the issues, but wondered out loud if her "job" might be threatened if the father became a more active parent.

You see, personal changes do not occur in a vacuum. As a consequence, fathers who act impulsively, and fail to adequately prepare for action, may set themselves up for bitter disappointment. Self changers learn, through experience, that taking time to prepare is essential.

The Action Stage

The Action Stage requires the greatest commitment of time and energy.

Fathers often equate this stage with goal attainment. Doing things differently is what it's all about, right? Well, the action stage is the most visible and many would guess that actual behavior change would get the most recognition.

Regrettably, many fathers report that changing superficial things on a temporary basis is not the same as changing deeply ingrained patterns of behavior. Lasting change requires large doses of support. But this support often fails to accompany change efforts either before or following a father's efforts to reconnect with his children.

Some fathers are slow to realize that sustaining important changes requires not only will power (i.e., commitment) but supporting and helping relationships as well. Many report disillusionment and rejection when their efforts to be "good dads" are not celebrated by their wives and children. Remember: Self changers are human, and we humans must learn how to create an environment that supports and rewards us. We cannot skip steps. When we shift into action and feel ignored or punished, chances are we will be "bumped" back to the contemplation phase. Honestly, it's probably going to happen anyway, but that does not mean we are not progressing. It may mean we are getting smarter.

HOW DO WE GET STARTED?

Finally...How do we get started?

Remember: when our emphasis is on self change, our passageway will always be through self awareness. To really get anywhere, we are going to have to drop our defenses and look seriously at the problems within our families and our roles in sustaining them.

If we're willing to acknowledge ways in which we've been absentee or critical dads, and to accept our responsibility for doing something about it, we've cleared the first hurdle. And even the best of fathers aren't always the best in every area of fathering. Over the past years, I've found that problems exist in almost all our families.

I understand that few of us get really excited about having problems. Most of us have enough to worry about without going out of our way to look for more problems to tackle. I've discovered however, that a close examination of our problems can point us in directions where change is most needed.

Stick with me here, because all this discussion is going somewhere important. As I've worked with families and talked with fathers, I've found that certain family problems seem to cluster. They overlap with each other.

WHERE DO WE START?

Think back the 13 contributions of fathers that we previously discussed. For example, think about Self Protection.

Now, consider what types of problems might crop up for a child whose father is unavailable to teach him or her about the importance of self protection. Such a child might lack assertiveness, show excessive fearfulness or become very dependent. Or they may have problems keeping up with their belongings. They might lose things, forget them or have them taken by other kids.

It is easy to see the ways in which these types of problems sort of "clump" together. It's also possible to see that a child from another family might not have these types of problems at all, yet portray other problems such as intense performance anxiety or a reluctance to take on challenging projects. We are all familiar with the type of youngster who quits too easily when frustrated.

I have matched each of the 13 fathering contributions to sets of commonly reported problems children experience within families. I've combined these problems with the self assessment questions that allow fathers to determine the need for personal change based on the types of problems their children are experiencing. Basically, I have designed a self assessment tool.

SELF ASSESSMENT

The assessment tool allows us to create our own personalized fathering profile.

The profile can tell us which of the contributions we are doing pretty well, as well as those on which we have fallen off track. The assessment profile will also indicate which of the fathering contributions we need to spend more time preparing for action and those for which we are already in the action stage.

So if you are willing, here is your opportunity to design your own action plan for successful fathering.

Start by taking a careful look at the assessment instrument and fill it out according to the instructions. Remember, the problems of our children can tell us a lot about ourselves as fathers. Drop your defenses and be honest with yourself.

Truly heroic fathers are not those for whom fathering comes easiest. Heroic dads are ordinary men, flawed men perhaps, who accept the challenges of fatherhood in spite of obstacles and past mistakes.

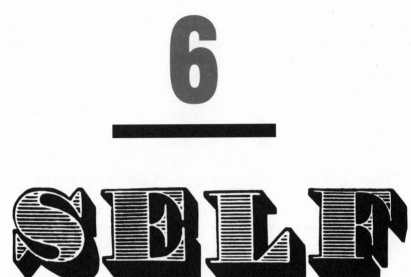

6

SELF

Assessment *Tool*

Self Assessment Tool

Here is an opportunity to rate yourself on the 13 Contributions of Successful Fathers we discussed. Take a look at the problems which sometimes indicate the need to work on a particular contribution. Remember, dads don't need to be perfect.

Once you have a fairly clear idea what the problem indicators are for each contribution, respond by choosing the most appropriate statement to assess the stage you are in for tackling a particular set of problems.

The answers (and the value of their scores) to the problem indicators will be one of the following:

1 = I am not sure I will ever take action.
2 = I intend to take action at some time beyond six months.
3 = I intend to take action in the next six months.
4 = I intend to take action in the next month.
5 = I have taken action on this problem within the past six months.
6 = I solved this problem more than six months ago.
7 = There has never been a problem in this area.

For the following questions, each of which indicates problems associated with the contributions, check the appropriate box to the right of the question. At the end of each "Contribution," you will be asked to total your score. This will help you assess where you stand in addressing each contribution.

In general terms, the scores by Contribution let you know where you stand for each of the contributions. Your scores will help you assess which aspect of the contribution may be worth pursuing first.

Now for the questions!

1 = I am not sure I will ever take action.
2 = I intend to take action at some time beyond the next six months.
3 = I intend to take action in the next six months.
4 = I intend to take action in the next month.
5 = I have taken action on this problem within the past six months.
6 = I solved this problem more than six months ago.
7 = There has never been a problem in this area.

FINANCIAL SUPPORT

1. Dad spends less than one hour *daily* with the child(ren) (individualized). _____
2. Most of the time Dad spends with the child(ren) is taking them to the movies or similar activities. _____
3. Work dominates all of Dad's available time. _____
4. Mom and Dad decided: He works, she raises the child(ren). _____
5. All my dad ever did was work, and that's what dads are suppose to do, isn't it? _____

Please total your score by adding your individual responses.

CARE GIVING

6. Dad doesn't help prepare meals, help with homework, make school visits, or attend to a sick child. _____
7. The child(ren) automatically take problems to mom. _____
8. My dad never did any of that stuff (prepare meals, help with homework, school visits etc.); it's not what men do. _____
9. She's the mother; that stuff (prepare meals, help with homework, school visits etc.), is her job! _____
10. Dad tries, but his wife (mother-in-law) seems to resent his intrusion. _____

Please total your score by adding your individual responses.

1 = I am not sure I will ever take action.
2 = I intend to take action at some time beyond the next six months.
3 = I intend to take action in the next six months.
4 = I intend to take action in the next month.
5 = I have taken action on this problem within the past six months.
6 = I solved this problem more than six months ago.
7 = There has never been a problem in this area.

TRUST

11. The child(ren) ignore or avoid Dad. _____
12. Dad always says "ask your mother." _____
13. Dad plays little, talks little. _____
14. Dad's time with the child(ren) is sporadic. _____
15. Dad avoids the hassle of kid stuff. _____

Please total your score by adding your individual responses.

IDENTITY

16. The child(ren) don't know Dad's "story". _____
17. The child(ren) don't go into his world and see Dad with other men or women. _____
18. The child(ren) don't know what Dad thinks. _____
19. The child(ren) don't see Dad taking role as parent (decision making). _____
20. Dad never initiates time alone with the child(ren). _____

Please total your score by adding your individual responses.

1 = I am not sure I will ever take action.
2 = I intend to take action at some time beyond the next six months.
3 = I intend to take action in the next six months.
4 = I intend to take action in the next month.
5 = I have taken action on this problem within the past six months.
6 = I solved this problem more than six months ago.
7 = There has never been a problem in this area.

FAMILY TRADITIONS

21. Dad leaves family traditions up to Mom. _____
22. Dad is confused where to start. _____
23. There are no traditions in our family that link Dad with the child(ren). _____
24. Dad enjoys doing a lot of things with his friends, but the child(ren) wouldn't enjoy yet. _____
25. Come to think about it, Dad has never considered the importance of family traditions. _____

Please total your score by adding your individual responses.

SECURITY

26. Dad never plays (rough house) with the child(ren). _____
27. Dad overreacts, gets angry and tends to yell a lot. _____
28. Dad leaves defers to Mom on all kid rearing issues including discipline. _____
29. The child(ren) are unclear about limits and that causes some behavioral problems. _____
30. The child(ren) are very "clingy" and dependent. _____

Please total your score by adding your individual responses.

1 = I am not sure I will ever take action.
2 = I intend to take action at some time beyond the next six months.
3 = I intend to take action in the next six months.
4 = I intend to take action in the next month.
5 = I have taken action on this problem within the past six months.
6 = I solved this problem more than six months ago.
7 = There has never been a problem in this area.

SELF PROTECTION

31. The child(ren) are fearful of bodily injury by others. _____
32. The child(ren) are overly shy and non-assertive
    (sometimes unable to speak for themselves). _____
33. The child(ren) lose possessions without consequences. _____
34. Others take the child(ren)'s stuff. _____
35. Dad avoids conflict with his wife. _____

Please total your score by adding your individual responses.

HUMOR

36. The child(ren) see Dad as humorless. _____
37. Dad is never playful with the child(ren). _____
38. We don't have any dad/kid jokes. _____
39. The child(ren) have problems being taught (coached) by
    Dad and Dad gets angry. _____
40. The child(ren) have a high level of anxiety about their
    performance and there is a high level of fear of failure. _____

Please total your score by adding your individual responses.

1 = I am not sure I will ever take action.
2 = I intend to take action at some time beyond the next six months.
3 = I intend to take action in the next six months.
4 = I intend to take action in the next month.
5 = I have taken action on this problem within the past six months.
6 = I solved this problem more than six months ago.
7 = There has never been a problem in this area.

COURAGE

41. The child(ren) are anxious about strangers. _____
42. The child(ren) are anxious about their performance. _____
43. The child(ren) avoid risk. _____
44. The child(ren) lack perseverance (want to quit when the "going gets tough"), and are easily discouraged with difficult tasks or whine to get out of situations that aren't comfortable. _____
45. Dad has difficulty "standing up" to his wife on issues that could trigger her anger. _____

Please total your score by adding your individual responses.

INDEPENDENCE

46. Mom does everything for the child(ren). _____
47. The child(ren) never earn anything (money or other items of value.) _____
48. The child(ren) are dependent on Mom to plan, protect, speak for them, and rescue them. _____
49. The child(ren) avoid experiences away from home. _____
50. The saying "Don't do anything for the child that they can do for themselves" doesn't fit our family. _____

Please total your score by adding your individual responses.

1 = I am not sure I will ever take action.
2 = I intend to take action at some time beyond the next six months.
3 = I intend to take action in the next six months.
4 = I intend to take action in the next month.
5 = I have taken action on this problem within the past six months.
6 = I solved this problem more than six months ago.
7 = There has never been a problem in this area.

SELF CONFIDENCE

51. Dad is the major critic around the house (difficult time praising). _____
52. Dad has a difficult time complementing the child(ren). _____
53. Dad fails to initiate activities which "test" the child(ren) (skills, risk-taking, etc.). _____
54. Dad is a poor teacher (e.g., doing things with the child(ren). _____
55. Dad has a difficult time just watching his child(ren); he always seems to "jump in". _____

Please total your score by adding your individual responses.

PATIENCE

56. When a child makes and error, Dad explodes. _____
57. Dad is easily disappointed or embarrassed by child(ren)'s performance. _____
58. Dad is unwilling to work with children and to to teach them complex skills, the children are not "natural" or "gifted". _____
59. When Dad attempts to initiate new activities, the child(ren) run the other way. _____
60. Dad can't seem to deal with situations in which his child(ren) doesn't share his opinions, likes or dislikes. _____

Please total your score by adding your individual responses.

1 = I am not sure I will ever take action.
2 = I intend to take action at some time beyond the next six months.
3 = I intend to take action in the next six months.
4 = I intend to take action in the next month.
5 = I have taken action on this problem within the past six months.
6 = I solved this problem more than six months ago.
7 = There has never been a problem in this area.

FORGIVENESS

61. Dad is unwilling to acknowledge his mistakes. _____
62. Dad blames Mom or child(ren) for problems but sidesteps doing anything about it, saying things like "You're the mother!" or "they just won't pay attention". _____
63. Dad yearns to be perfect, but secretly fears his own fathering capabilities. _____
64. Child(ren) are caught telling lies to avoid acknowledging their mistakes or poor judgment. _____
65. Dad made lots of mistakes as a kid, but would never tell his child(ren) that he was anything but an ideal child. _____

Please total your score by adding your individual responses.

Please turn to page 132.

Transcribe the total scores for each Contribution into the boxes below:

Financial Support........ ☐   Humor......................... ☐

Caregiving................... ☐   Courage...................... ☐

Trust............................ ☐   Independence.............. ☐

Identity....................... ☐   Self Confidence........... ☐

Family Traditions....... ☐   Patience...................... ☐

Security....................... ☐   Forgiveness................. ☐

Self Protection............. ☐

If your score is	You are in stage
31-35	Maintenance
26-30	Action
21-25	Planning
16-20	Contemplation
11-15	Pre-contemplation
5-10	Not yet committed

Now, plot your total scores on the following page by shading in the 13 columns with the corresponding total score. This chart will help you to visualize your personal Successful Fathering profile.

Successful Fathering Self Assessment Profile

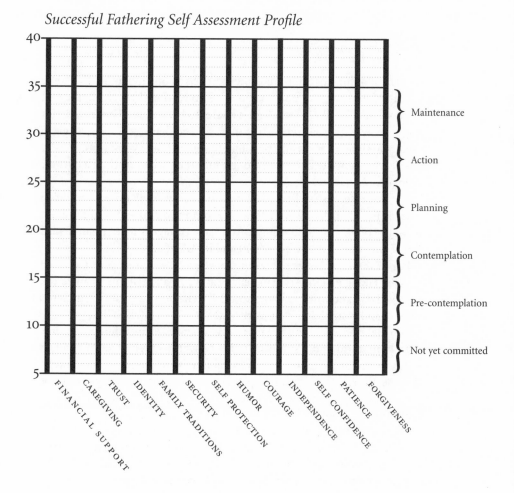

USING YOUR PROFILE

In this final section of the book, let's focus on your self assessed scores that fall within the Contemplation, Preparation or Action Stages. Take a look at your profile and take note of which of your scores fall within the Contemplation stage. This is where we'll begin. But before we do, let me recommend if you want a more thorough understanding of the stages of personal change described here, that you check out *Changing for Good,* by James Prochaska and his colleagues. For now though, let's focus on how you can benefit from this information.

The Contemplation Stage

I've tried to think of a less imposing word than contemplation. I've come up with deliberate and ponder. I don't know, when I get stuck, the best word seems a lot like "worry." As it relates to becoming a better Dad, this stage involves 1) an awareness that there are problems, and 2) a struggle to understand their causes and possible solutions. Many young fathers who didn't have active dads as role models find themselves stuck in a chronic state of ambivalence.

The issue here is readiness. That is, not being ready for action. Being stuck is not all bad, however. Talking about problems and reading about them are often crucial first steps. At least this stage is better than denial. Contemplation is vitally important and it's often hard work.

For example, an essential task is to weight the "Pros" and "Cons" of actually taking action. Ask yourself, "Can I actually call myself an active, involved dad and work 70 hours a week?" What are the positive outcomes for you and your child if you work less? Seriously....Make a list.

Next take a look at the negative consequences of spending more time with your child and less at work. That's right. These types of changes don't occur in a vacuum. Factors such as your career advancement, income, the reaction of your employer or supervisor or your wife must be considered before change can successfully be made. I've learned that premature action sometimes backfires when men act impulsive.

You've got to ask the right questions. Define your goals and collect the right kinds of information. We're talking about long term, meaningful change. This demands that we feel emotionally pumped up about the need to do something different, but not to go off half-cocked.

So you must think before you act. Will you have the support of your wife? Do both of you know what is likely to change when you change? One man I know quit a well paying job which required him to travel 250 days a year to be a better family man. His wife filed for divorce because it meant she could no longer remain at home as a full time mom. Think and ask questions, don't assume anything!

The Preparation Stage

If you discover that some of your scores fall in the preparation stage, read this section very carefully. This stage is absolutely crucial and it is the one most of us want to rush through and shortcut. We want to get into action. But wait!

Preparation readies us to not only take action, but to handle unexpected roadblocks to our success. I can tell you from years of experience that it is these unanticipated challenges that derail premature attempts at change. Long term change often requires that we acquire new skills and roundup the resources we'll need when the going gets tough.

Preparation moves us from gathering information about the problem to the identification of the specific steps needed to solve the problem. At this stage, we've shifted from being worried about not changing to thinking about ways to insure our success. This is a very different process. Planning looks a lot like a dress rehearsal for the future. Through planning, we begin to gain confidence about what we're about to attempt.

We must say what we intend to do. Going public is a testament to our level of commitment and a key step in solidifying our will power. In a sense, it puts others on notice and is a way of recruiting support and helping relationships.

In this stage, there is a noticeable shift not only in our perception of the importance of the "cons" versus the "pros" of changing, but also the number of "pros" begin to increase. Specifically, make a list of the pros and cons of changing your behavior as a father. Before you are ready to move from Preparation into the Action stage, the number of pros should definitely outweigh the cons.

Now is the time to enlist supporters as well as sources of wisdom and experience. Typically, the initial stages of the Action stage are very stressful. You'll profit from having encouraging and problem solving allies to keep your will power high.

The Action Stage

Here are some important reminders you'll need to keep in mind. First, premature action is often a source of major disappointment. However, setbacks can be used as valuable sources of information in rebuilding your game plan. Remember, many successful self changers recycled from the Preparation to Action stage four or five times before they were successful.

Helping relationships are vital. Becoming an active, involved father has seldom been accomplished by attempting to go it on one's own. One of the functions of the Preparation Stage is to identify allies and sources of support. Don't underestimate the value of social reinforcement in sustaining difficult changes. You must know who your friends are and be prepared to use them as resources when necessary.

Avoid what I call *"fear talk"*. Change triggers anxiety. As the time for changes approaches, our anxiety escalates. When we get caught up in our anxious feelings, our thoughts automatically become negative and our self confidence drops like a stone. Learn to catch yourself when you slip into fear talk. Be prepared to shut it off and replace it with a more realistic and less fearful view of yourself.

If you can, for each problem behavior, come up with a substitute, positive fathering behavior. I've found it is more difficult to stop problem behaviors when we don't know ahead of time what we're going to do instead. Intending to just *"not do"* problem behaviors is often reflective of poor planning. For example, make a list of alternative positive behaviors which you intend to replace being critical or spending every evening on your computer, or spending every weekend at the office.

Make being an active father your top priority. Think about your dad or the dad you wished you'd had. Are you willing to be come the dad you needed as a kid? The dad your kid needs? You're the guy for the job. Best wishes Sport!

Notes

Wade Horn, Ph.D., *Father Facts* (Lancaster, PA; The National Fatherhood Initiative, 1995).

John Gray, Ph.D., *Men are from Mars, Women are from Venus,* (New York; Harper Collins, 1992).

M. Scott Peck, Ph.D., *The Road Less Traveled,* (New York; Simon and Schuster, 1978).

James Prochaska, Ph.D., *Changing for Good,* (New York NY; William Morrow and Company).

N. Victoria Secunda, *Women and Their Families,* (New York; Delacorte Press, 1992).

Ronald L. Klinger, Ph.D.

Dr. Ron Klinger has dedicated much of the past decade researching fathering issues. He regularly conducts workshops where participants learn to understand the father's role within the family. A nationally respected pioneer in this area, Dr. Klinger is the author of *The Common Sense No-Frills, Plain-English Guide to Being A Successful Dad.* He has made fathering presentations for numerous organizations including the Texas Attorney General's office, Round Rock Independent School District, U. S. Department of Health and Human Services, National Fatherhood Initiative, and the Indiana Governor's Conference on Fatherhood.

Father of a teenage son, Dr. Klinger earned his doctorate from the University of Texas at Austin and is a licensed psychologist in the State of Texas. He is the founding President of the Center for Successful Fathering.

Through the Center for Successful Fathering, Dr. Klinger has created curriculum offered to schools, professionals and directly to fathers. It is also the basis for continuing education seminars taught to mental health professionals. "Accepting the Challenges of Fatherhood" is a six-part program aimed at the fathers (or potential fathers) of children from birth through elementary school ages.

Gay Klinger, M.S.

A practicing therapist for more than seven years, Gay Klinger shares a successful counseling practice with her husband, Ron Klinger, Ph.D. She is mother of their son and specializes in working with families, groups, adolescents and women on relationship issues.

Working with her husband, she has developed the Lake Travis Challenge Course, a facility where participants learn about themselves and others while enhancing communication, problem-solving and cooperation skills. Her previous experience includes more than 18 years of teaching and staff development for public schools in California and Texas.

Gay holds a master's degree in Special Education from California State University at Fullerton (1973) and completed 30 graduate hours in counseling at Southwest Texas State, San Marcos (1988). She is also a Licensed Professional Counselor (L.P.C.) and a Certified Imago Relationship Counselor.

140